Guerrilla
Hostage

Guerrilla
Hostage

810 Days in Captivity

Denise Marie Siino

 Fleming H. Revell
A Division of Baker Book House
Grand Rapids, Michigan 49516

Published by Fleming H. Revell
a division of Baker Book House Company
P.O. Box 6287, Grand Rapids, MI 49516-6287

Printed in the United States of America

Library of Congress Cataloging-in-Publication Data

Siino, Denise Marie, 1958–
    Guerrilla hostage : 810 days in captivity / Denise Marie Siino.
        p.   cm.
    Includes bibliographical references.
    ISBN 0-8007-5693-2 (pbk.)
        1. Rising, Ray—Captivity, 1994–1996. 2. Hostages—Colombia—
Biography. 3. Hostages—United States—Biography. 4. Summer Institute
of Linguistics—Biography. I. Title.
    BV2372.R47S55   1999
    278.61'0829'092—dc21   98-42893

Unless otherwise indicated, Scripture quotations are from the HOLY BIBLE, NEW INTERNATIONAL VERSION®. NIV®. Copyright © 1973, 1978, 1984 by International Bible Society. Used by permission of Zondervan Publishing House. All rights reserved.

Scripture quotations identified KJV are from the King James Version of the Bible.

Scripture quotations identified NASB are from the NEW AMERICAN STANDARD BIBLE®, Coyright © The Lockman Foundation 1960, 1962, 1963, 1968, 1971, 1972, 1973, 1975, 1977, 1995. Used by permission.

Scripture quotations identified NKJV are from the New King James Version. Copyright © 1979, 1980, 1982 by Thomas Nelson, Inc. Used by permission. All rights reserved.

Scripture quotations identified TLB are from *The Living Bible* © 1971. Used by permission of Tyndale House Publishers, Inc., Wheaton, IL 60189. All rights reserved.

With the exception of Ray Rising and his family, the Stendal family, and Chester Bitterman and the five New Tribes missionaries referred to in chapters 7 and 9, all the names of individuals identified in this book have been changed. This has been done to protect them from any difficulties or harm stemming from their involvement in helping secure Ray's freedom. Also, the details of the agreement leading to Ray's release have not been included in the book in order to avoid interfering in any way with the ongoing investigation regarding the three New Tribes missionaries still believed to be held by guerrilla factions in Colombia.

For current information about all releases from Baker Book House, visit our web site:
http://www.bakerbooks.com

Contents

Preface   7

Acknowledgments   11

Introduction:
Beginnings   13

1 Kidnapped!   25
  March 31, 1994

  The Crisis
  Committee   38
  March 31 to April 1994

  Alone
  and Unsettled   41
  April 1994

2 The Calling   43
  April to July 1994

  First Contact   61
  June to July 1994

  Negotiations   64
  June to September 1994

3 Looking Death
  in the Eye   69
  July to October 1994

  Terrible News   83
  August to December 1994

4 Beside the River   85
  October to November 1994

  Dead or Alive?   93
  December 1994

  Christmas
  Greetings   95
  December 1994

5 The Holidays   107
  *December 1994
  to January 1995*

  Hope   119
  January 1995

6 To Church   121
  January to February 1995

7 Ups and Downs   135
  February to June 1995

  Airdrop   149
  February 1995

  Alive and Well   151
  May to June 1995

8 Justice and Mercy   153
  June to November 1995

9 Deadly Games   167
  *November 1995
  to February 1996*

Contents

Garbled Messages   179
December 1995

Difficult Times   181
January to March 1996

10 The Long Haul   187
March to May 1996

Final Proof   198
May to June 1996

A Deal   201
June 1996

11 Release!   203
June 16–17, 1996

Good News!   214
June 11–17, 1996

Conclusion:
Illuminating
the Path   217

Epilogue   225

Afterword   229

Appendix: List
of Names   231

Notes   233

6

Preface

Give me such love for God and men, as will blot out all hatred and bitterness.

Dietrich Bonhoeffer

When I first heard about Ray Rising's liberation on June 17, 1996, after he had been held captive by Colombian guerrillas for over twenty-six months, I was curious what his feelings were toward his captors. Human nature, left to its own devices, would suggest a cold bitterness that could devour a lifetime, yet the little bit of news I'd heard indicated that Ray harbored no ill will. *How could that be?* I wondered.

Years ago, I was confronted by an intruder in my home early one morning. As a Christian I knew God's mandate to love my enemy, but I had been unable to apply it to my personal life; there were no "handles" to grasp on to. Over time, the fear of those minutes had turned into antagonism, even hatred, and I was crippled in its grip. I knew if I ever met my adversary again, words such as *love* and *forgiveness* would not even cross my mind, let alone my lips.

I was fascinated by Ray's story, and knew I *had* to write about it. At the time I thought my goal was to communicate a remarkable story to the world in a way that embraced Ray's faith and service to God, but looking back now I realize my yearning to tell the story went deeper than that. I wanted to know how Ray was able to hurdle his anger and love his enemies, and how I could do the same. Little did I know what my August 1996 article for the *L.A. Times* would open up!

Several months after the article came out, the idea of a book blossomed, paving the way for further dialogue with Ray. I eventually spent a week working closely with Ray and his wife, Doris, at their home in Waxhaw, North Carolina. In a way that is impossible to relate here, while sitting at their kitchen table my malice toward my own personal "monster" disintegrated in an afternoon of tears, prayer, and laughter. That day I discovered that my assailant was not my real enemy, rather it was the fear that lurked within my heart—fear of manipulation and injury, of what I could not see or understand. Listening to Ray share his experiences and lessons of overcoming fear in a hostile environment, I learned afresh how to trust God and overcome my own trepidations.

As believers in the Prince of Peace, we do not have the luxury of viewing any one of God's creation through the lens of mere human sentiment. Instead, we are to honor God by affirming that all humanity is created in his image, *including* our enemies. A tall order, I know. But as our culture changes and values swing away from our Judeo-Christian roots, I'm convinced it's a lesson we must learn to understand fully the calling of God in our lives and to be effective witnesses to the world around us.

So how do we respond to those who wish to remove "In God We Trust" from our currency and "under God" from our pledge? To the individuals who defy the God of the

Bible and the people who are called by his name? To a society that demands tolerance toward actions and lifestyles that God calls sin? How do we respond? By being a people set apart, standing up for what we believe in public and behind closed doors, without compromise or excuse, all the while being respectful and compassionate, as Christ was to a hurting world blinded by Satan, the Father of Lies.

Sound impossible? So I thought not long ago; so Ray might have thought before being swooped away into a communist guerrilla camp where he sometimes faced ridicule and antagonism, even fear of death, in part because he placed his trust in God and lived day by day according to what he believed.

Few of us will ever wind up in a communist guerrilla camp, but all of us, in some form or another, will experience misunderstanding, rejection, perhaps even animosity if we hold fast to and proclaim our biblical beliefs. Jesus said it would be so. But God is trustworthy and will strengthen and guide us and uplift us when we fall. And as we strive to pursue God and walk in integrity, we will experience God's presence in a way that is more real, more intimate than we ever imagined possible.

Ray Rising did. Here is his incredible story.

Acknowledgments

I am indebted to many people, without whom this book would have been impossible to write. Primarily, thanks to the only true and living God, who above all others deserves my thanks and praise for using this story in a very special way in my own life. To him be all glory and honor!

To my husband, Jack, who has faithfully trusted God in encouraging me to pursue my passion; and to my kids, Joel and Amy, who have listened to God with open minds and hearts and willingly submitted their own wills to his throughout this writing process. I praise God for the love we share.

To Ray and Doris Rising for sharing their very personal and dramatic story with me and for becoming my good friends as well. I cherish every moment we have spent together. May God bless all your future endeavors in his service.

To the many individuals at Wycliffe, SIL, and JAARS—in Bogotá and the States—who spent hours upon hours scouring through their memories, notes, and the crisis archives on my behalf and prayed for this project from conception to completion. Special thanks to Arthur Lightbody, who made my initial contact with Ray possible and helped me along the way.

To Russell and Chaddy Stendal for bringing Colombia to life for me.

To Quil Lawrence, journalist for National Public Radio, for helping me understand the political climate in Colombia.

To Joan Springhetti, *Times Orange County* editor, for her patience and willingness to teach me how to find the focus of a good story.

To Ana Wood for her friendship and assistance in verifying the Spanish used throughout the text.

To my friends at the Orange Writer's Circle for their wonderful support.

To Ken Wales and the Flower Man for their wise counsel and faith in my abilities and for opening doors to help further my professional career.

To Peggy McAulay and Susan LaFlamme for their listening ears and fervent prayers.

Introduction

Beginnings

> To the Europeans, South America is a man with a moustache, a guitar, and a gun. . . . They don't understand the problem.
>
> Gabriel García Márquez,
> *No One Writes to the Colonel*

Long ago, when the only "guerrillas" (spelled differently) in existence were the large, hairy apes living in equatorial Africa, Colombia reigned as a garden paradise in the magical, little-understood land of South America. With coastlines on two oceans, a rich, topographically diverse interior, and much-treasured natural resources, Colombia captured the hearts and minds of the Spanish conquistadors.[1] First settled in 1509, by the mid-1500s most of the country's interior had been conquered, with Santafé de Bogotá (Bogotá) as its capital. The area became known as the Spanish colony of New Granada.

For the next two hundred and fifty years, little changed except the number of Latins leaving the Old World for the new one. In 1810, these expatriates—happy in their new home but disgruntled with Spain's iron grip—began their

13

struggle for independence against the motherland. In 1812, a Venezuelan named Simón Bolívar led the revolution, and in 1819, the independent republic of Gran Colombia was born. Ruled by Bolívar and Francisco Santander, it included the present-day countries of Colombia, Ecuador, Panama, and Venezuela. By 1830, however, the republic had deteriorated, with Colombia (including Panama), Ecuador, and Venezuela becoming independent states. This period saw the birth of liberal and conservative political parties all across South America; in Colombia they comprised the followers of Bolívar (liberal) and Santander (conservative). Like modern-day democrats and republicans, these two warring groups stood nose to nose in the competition for power.

During the rest of the nineteenth century, continuing rivalry between the liberals and the conservatives resulted in isolated armed conflict throughout the land. In those days as in current times, the capital city was something of a barometer for Colombia, and, much like the rest of the country, Bogotá retained a calm that belied the pervading violence. On an efflorescent plateau high in the Andes, its streets lined with bougainvillea and scented with eucalyptus, the quiet city lay. But while women with long, black plaits of hair dangling down their backs led donkey-drawn carts and sold their produce among the quaint colonial neighborhoods, a political storm gathered just outside the city's mountain peak borders. The populace did not know how to deal with the tumult; many ignored it, hoping it would go away. *"Aqui no pasa nada,"* "Nothing happens here,"[2] they said.

But something did happen: Civil war broke out in 1899 and lasted until 1903. At the same time, Panama rebelled and achieved its independence from Colombia (with the help of the United States due to its interests in the Panama Canal Zone). Even after the war ended, conflict between the liberals and the conservatives continued, with a bloody

14

uprising in the north coast town of Cienega in 1928, over a banana workers strike, punctuating the violence. For the next twenty years, Colombia balanced precariously between the proverbial match and stick of dynamite.

In 1948, the dynamite finally exploded. Jorge Eliecer Gaitán, a great radical leader beloved by the common people, was assassinated on the street outside his office in Bogotá. A lawyer who dreamed of introducing true pluralistic, issues-oriented politics to Colombia, his death triggered another more deadly civil war. Dubbed *La Violencia,* the war lasted from 1948 to 1957 and killed nearly three hundred thousand people. In the midst of this, in 1953, a military coup occurred, and General Gustavo Rojas Pinilla became dictator of the country. His reign of terror was short lived, however, as the two warring parties united temporarily in opposition to Pinilla's heavy-handed regime.

In 1957, after the overthrow of Pinilla, the liberals and the conservatives agreed to form the National Front, in which the presidency would alternate between candidates from the two parties every four years while all other offices would be divided equally. In 1974, this form of government was replaced by open elections for all public offices (the maximum length of office is still four years).

Meanwhile, a student at the National University in Bogotá, Cuban-born Fidel Castro, began propagating Marxist/Leninist ideology among the students there. Others followed suit in universities throughout the country. After returning to his homeland, Castro seized power in Havana as prime minister of Cuba in 1959, overthrowing the U.S.-backed dictatorship of Fulgencio Batista. He established a socialist state with the aid of the communist U.S.S.R. and became the new official "president" of Cuba in 1976. During this time, back in Colombia, hundreds of college students and *campesinos* (rural people)—angered by the "closed democracy"[3] and influenced by Marxist doctrine and other thought—began

15

organizing into groups and rebelling against the government. Eventually, these became the armed guerrilla forces of the modern era, each one founded on a different ideology. The primary groups were the ELN (National Liberation Army), EPL (Popular Liberation Army), FARC (the Revolutionary Armed Forces of Colombia), and M-19 (M stands for "Movement," and 19 is in commemoration of April 19, 1970, when the presidential candidate of a populist opposition movement who was two million votes ahead was bought off and the conservative candidate was installed, killing—in the minds of the revolutionaries—any hope of achieving change through the electoral process). Originally modeled after and subsidized by communist Russia and Cuba, the FARC is the oldest and largest of all the guerrilla forces.

At first the guerrillas' influence on the rural areas of the country was intoxicating. Their common goal being the redistribution of land at a time when 5 percent of the population owned 90 percent of the held property, they presented themselves as liberators who would free the poor and politically unrepresented from the oppression of the elite ruling factions. But as the *campesinos* observed the areas where the guerrillas exerted their control, the tide of popular opinion slowly shifted. Business owners, ranchers, and farmers were "taxed" heavily for protection against common criminals, extortion became routine, and the execution of "undesirables" commonplace.[4] The government (through political means) and especially the military tried opposing these forces but found the going slow. Whereas the guerrillas generally ran around in bands of little more than a dozen or two at a time and could maneuver through the *llanos*[5] and jungles with relative ease, the military with its troops of one hundred or more found tactics in these areas extremely difficult.

Initially the guerrillas followed their ideologies with a purity and zeal that made their founders proud. But with time, these ideals changed, and as funding for the various groups dwindled,[6] new means for increasing revenue began to be explored. The drug explosion of the 1960s and 1970s, along with Colombia's position as a significant grower of marijuana, coca, and poppies, not only fueled the fire but introduced a new objective as well.[7] As the guerrilla organizations "grew up," their need for survival and comfort at least equaled their political goal of taking over the country with their doctrines. As Jaime Bateman, founder of the M-19, had been known to say: "The revolution is not just about having enough to eat, it's about being able to eat what we like."[8] With this new objective came a renewed fervor to protect and nurture the guerrilla "family" at all costs.

In the 1970s, political kidnappings and kidnappings of the commoner and foreigner for ransom blossomed into another avenue of income. By the early 1980s, with kidnapping insurance in place for thousands of political figures as well as national and international corporate executives, the practice had become a full-blown moneymaking venture.[9]

As the conflict between the guerrillas and the military intensified, corruption and extraordinary acts of brutality erupted on all sides. The zenith of these events included the general amnesty granted the two largest guerrilla forces by the government in 1983 (many, generally known as the *Unión Patriótica,* did lay down their weapons at this time); the large number of murders, sustained by the guerrillas, that followed; and the invasion of the Palace of Justice (equal to the U.S.'s Supreme Court) by thirty-five M-19 guerrillas in 1985 in an effort to force the justices to place the government on trial for its supposed misconduct. This assault on the palace and the subsequent taking of hostages met with tremendous firepower on the part of the military. Within two days, the building was demolished, and most of the guerrillas and many of the civilians (including eleven justices) who were working at the time of the takeover were dead.

This single event marked the symbolic end of one type of war between the government, military, and guerrillas and the beginning of another—the "Dirty War" as it has since been called. In this new war, which now includes a relatively new player, the auto-defense units,[10] all sides are guilty of the wooing and annihilation of multitudes of Colombians each year, through legitimate as well as illegitimate means. Further, the Dirty War is typified by clandestine efforts to conceal and in some cases expedite impunity for parties responsible for violent acts. The following figures collected by the Data Bank of the Inter-Congregational Commission of Peace and Justice in Colombia suggest the magnitude the violence has reached:[11]

Victims of Political Violence in Colombia, 1988–1995

Political assassinations	6,177
Assassinations presumed to be political	10,556
Assassinations presumed to be "social cleansing"	2,459
Deaths in combat between army and guerrillas	9,140
People forcibly disappeared*	1,451
Obscure assassinations**	37,595
Total:	**67,378**
Average per month:	**701.9**
Average per day:	**23.4**

*When a person is abducted and never heard from again and no one claims responsibility for the disappearance.

**Killings for which no motive is clearly identified when the murder is registered. This number does not include deaths caused by personal disputes or crimes committed by private individuals.

What these numbers fail to show is the ever increasing intensity of bedlam the country sustains with each passing year. The majority of this damage is borne in the countryside as the military, guerrillas, and auto-defenses battle for control of these areas one municipality at a time. In these provincial towns, business goes on in time-honored fashion, yet there is a lackluster to the hubbub of everyday living as each waking moment is infused with fear and oppression. Unfortunately, there is little for most of the people to do but make the best of the situation.

Even in the capital city, where security is greatest, the violence continues to take its toll. The Bogotá of the 1990s exudes little of the charm and tranquility that previously graced the city. The thin mountain air now smells as much of exhaust as piquant eucalyptus, and the donkey carts—now bearing recyclable materials toward the nearest collection center—scurry to make their way through the thousands of motorists heading in every direction. As if emphasizing the disheartened spirit of the city, few of the sidewalk flower stands that once accented the city streets like the spots on dotted swiss fabric remain. The few enduring shops, still-exquisite splashes of vibrant color amid the dull facades of the metropolis, are now supplied by greenhouses instead of the burgeoning vistas of color that once adorned the plateau.[12] The colonial neighborhoods, demolished in the wake of two civil wars, have been replaced by multistory apartment buildings under double lock and key and surveyed by unmarked security guards. Indeed, an entire segment of the city in the northern quadrant is patrolled by armed guards. This northern "zone," as it is called, is considered the safest in Bogotá and is where most foreign executives and businessmen live and work. From there the zones generally deteriorate in terms of safety as the city sprawls southward. On one street dubbed *Calle Bala,* or "Bullet Street," by city dwellers, it is said that one can hire an assassin for a mere twenty dollars.

Yet, for all the hostility, the vast majority of Colombians are gracious and gentle, albeit guarded. Outside the haven of their homes—wherein they may speculate over the facts of this uprising or that clash—they speak little of affairs going on throughout their land. Shell-shocked, it's business as usual in Colombia. *Aqui no pasa nada.*

19

It is in this environment that members of the Summer Institute of Linguistics (SIL)[13] have lived and worked in Colombia for the last thirty-four years. SIL founder William Cameron Townsend, nicknamed "Uncle Cam" by his many friends, first contacted the Colombian government in 1953, requesting that his organization be allowed into the country to bring literacy to the many indigenous groups living in its vast jungle and mountainous regions. In 1962, he signed a contract with government officials, and in 1964, the first several dozen translators and support personnel moved into SIL's two primary Colombian headquarters in Bogotá and Lomalinda, a rural center nearly two hundred miles to the southeast. But this event did not mark the birth of SIL, whose beginnings go back nearly sixty-five years.

As a young man struggling to finance his education at Occidental College in Los Angeles, California, near the end of World War I, Uncle Cam decided to take a year off to sell Spanish Bibles in Central America. In 1917, he boarded a steamer headed for Guatemala, then traveled on foot and by mule through the backwoods of that untamed land, his target audience the many tribal Indians found deep in its jungle interior. But when he found them he discovered a startling truth: Very few could understand, much less read, the Spanish language. In fact, with few exceptions, their own mother tongues had been passed down orally from generation to generation and had no written form. The precious books he so arduously carried for hundreds of miles were totally useless to them.

One pointed conversation with a resident from the local population, in particular, clarified the significance of the dilemma: "If your God is so great," the man asked, "why doesn't he speak my language?" *Indeed, why doesn't he?* Uncle Cam wondered. From that point forward a dream crystallized in his mind: to bring the Word of God to those who do not have it in their "heart language."[14]

The first step toward this goal was to learn their language—in this case Cakchiquel, a derivative of the ancient Mayan language—then devise an alphabet, and finally, translate the New Testament into it.[15] Twelve years later, the monumental task was complete and the first New Testament in the Cakchiquel language was presented to the president of Guatemala. Meanwhile, Uncle Cam had founded five schools, a clinic, a print shop, and an orphanage to meet the needs of the indigenous population.

At that time, it was believed that potentially one thousand languages existed in Central and South America that had no written form.[16] Was it possible to spearhead a movement to bring literacy and the Word of God to each one of them? In 1934, Uncle Cam returned to the United States to begin a program aimed at doing just that. Soon, a summer training camp for prospective Bible translators—Camp Wycliffe (named after the Englishman, John Wycliffe, who first translated the Scriptures into the English language)—was born in an Arkansas farmhouse with two students showing up for that first round of classes.[17] In 1935, Uncle Cam led a group of young people into Mexico to begin the first SIL study program of the various indigenous languages there. Among this initial group of translators was a man named Kenneth Pike, who later became president of SIL, holding the post until retirement in 1978.[18]

In 1942, in response to the growing need to financially and in other ways support the SIL personnel, Wycliffe Bible Translators was founded. Currently headquartered in Huntington Beach, California, Wycliffe USA communicates the need for Bible translation in people's heart languages and provides the resources needed to accomplish that task through personnel, finances, and prayer.

Throughout his years of travel, Uncle Cam often wished for the "wings of a bird" to whisk him to the many locations that God called him to. He occasionally took advantage of

21

flight service offered by the nationals of a foreign land. In 1947, Uncle Cam and his wife, Elaine, were injured in a plane wreck in Mexico. During his healing process, Cam realized the need for trained and experienced personnel who could navigate the difficult jungle and mountain terrains so common to Central and South America. Within a year, JAARS (originally an acronym for Jungle Aviation and Radio Service) was born, its first plane a surplus U.S. Marine Grumman Duck, and its first pilot a woman by the name of Betty Greene. For the past fifty years JAARS, headquartered in Waxhaw, North Carolina, has supported Bible translators and technical personnel with flight and electronic communication service, as well as computer technology, purchasing, shipping, and other services, the world over.

Ray Rising's connection to Colombia is almost as old as SIL's. As a youngster growing up in Baudette, Minnesota, Ray loved ham radios and knew he wanted to work in the field of radio communications some day. As a teenager in the 1950s, he read with interest a *Reader's Digest* article titled "2000 Tongues to Go" about Wycliffe's work of Bible translation with indigenous peoples worldwide and their need for electronics specialists. He wrote Wycliffe a letter explaining his interest in their program. Sensing through further correspondence Ray's youth and lack of Christian experience, Wycliffe recommended he wait a while before proceeding with any plans toward missions work.

In July 1961, after graduating from high school the previous year, Ray attended a Billy Graham crusade in St. Paul and gave his heart to Jesus Christ. He began attending a local electronics trade school and again contacted Wycliffe. This time they responded with interest, suggesting that he attend a Bible college for a year. It was at Oak Hills Bible Institute in Bemidji, Minnesota, that Ray met his wife, Doris. In 1964 they married, and in June of 1965 they signed up for the SIL training course in Norman, Oklahoma.

Following this six-week program, Ray and Doris went to Waxhaw, North Carolina, for three months of specialized orientation[19] followed by another three months of jungle camp in the state of Chiapas, Mexico, near the Guatemalan border. There, amid a sometimes inhospitable environment, they and several dozen other SIL members experienced what life would be like out in the field and what it meant to carry the Word of God to the ends of the earth.[20]

In October 1966, two years after Lomalinda's founding, Ray and Doris headed for their new home at the SIL translation facility deep in the heart of Colombia. As Lomalinda was the main traffic hub for all SIL radio communications, Ray's post involved improving transmissions between Bogotá and Lomalinda and between Lomalinda and the translators in their village locations. Another responsibility entailed tracking flight information of the JAARS aircraft flying around the country.

Sensing a lack of interaction between himself and the world outside Lomalinda's boundaries, in 1975, Ray joined a ham radio club in Villavicencio, where he was able to get to know the Colombian people—many of whom were local professionals in various occupations—firsthand. By this time both of his sons had been born, Ray Jr. in 1969 and Rollin in 1975, and Ray immersed himself in the lives of young people, specifically by heading up (with another father) the Boys' Brigade.

After eleven years in Colombia, Ray and Doris left in 1977 for Ecuador, where Ray worked to install telephone communications links among the SIL centers there. After completion of this project and a furlough in the States, they returned to Lomalinda in 1983, where Ray worked on a similar telephone project between Bogotá and Lomalinda. He also returned to the ham radio club. This contact afforded him the opportunity to build friendships with the Colombian people during a time when SIL was experiencing a great deal of erroneous publicity from the local media, as well as skepticism from the army and the local people.[21]

As time passed, Ray's success in forming bonds with these Colombians gave way to a new opportunity and responsibility at Lomalinda—that of public relations and security. In these roles it was his job to welcome visitors into the center, serve as a liaison between Lomalinda and the provincial army base, and promote healthy relations between SIL and local and federal government officials, including elevating an understanding of SIL's work in the country.

Over the next ten years, Ray's connections with these official contacts evolved into friendships with the common folk, specifically those living in the small town of Puerto Lleras.[22] Seeing the hopelessness of its battle-worn and broken residents, Ray made an effort to befriend many, especially the poorest and most needy within the community. Representing Lomalinda, he frequently brought food to hungry families and offered financial support to young boys and girls whose parents could not afford the supplies necessary for an education (shoes, uniforms, and books). He befriended boys and girls of all ages, sometimes becoming a father to the fatherless and lending emotional support where needed. Once he took a young boy to a local bullfight; on another occasion he helped find a home for a girl who had no place to go.

Although these and many other activities resulted in a better association between SIL and the government, the army, and the local Colombians, Ray's efforts went virtually unnoticed by the local guerrillas, who saw Lomalinda as nothing more than an American base with nice homes, running water, and electricity—an oasis of capitalist wealth in their midst. As the weeks passed, many watchful eyes took notice of Ray as he drove the near-deserted road between Puerto Lleras and Lomalinda. At night, as the daily breezes subsided, the jungle itself seemed to whisper his name.

1

Kidnapped!

March 31, 1994

> You prepare a table before me in
>   the presence of my enemies;
> You anoint my head with oil;
> My cup runs over.
>
> Psalm 23:5 NKJV

Ray Rising awoke early the morning of Maundy Thursday, 1994, to a dreary sky, as the sun tried to force its way through a layer of clouds above the horizon of the rolling hills of Lomalinda. It was a holiday in *Colombia—Semana Santa,* or Holy Week—so he decided to close his eyes and sleep a while longer, at least until the sun chased away the gloom.

When he woke up again it was eight o'clock and quite bright outside. As his wife, Doris, prepared breakfast, Ray showered and dressed in a pair of blue jeans and a button-down striped shirt, and ran a comb through his chestnut brown hair. Then sitting down at the kitchen table set with juice, bacon, eggs, and toast, he took Doris's hand and said grace.

"Remember that guy I told you about—Vincent—who I've been buying school supplies from?" Ray said as Doris bit into a piece of toast. "A group of us are going to meet him at his farm across the lake for lunch today, about 12:30. Rollin's coming along."

"Are the girls invited too?"

"Nope, just us men." Ray smiled and patted her arm. "But I want to go into Puerto Lleras when I get back. Want to come along?"

"No, I'd just as soon stay here. It's supposed to be hot today. Are you remembering the radio department potluck tonight?"

"What time is that?"

"Seven."

"I'll be back by then."

After breakfast, Ray relaxed and puttered around the house until 11:30, then drove down to the lake, where a motorboat bobbed up and down next to a homemade dock. When everyone was accounted for they headed across the lake, arriving on the other side at 12:30. After tying the boat to a tree near the water's edge, Ray and his companions trudged up the *loma* (hill) toward the farmhouse.

As his friends went ahead, Ray stopped and looked back toward Lomalinda. It wasn't often he got to see the translation center from this vantage point, and shielding his face from the hot sun with his hand, he looked out over the shimmering water at the house-topped hills on the other side. A couple of the citrus trees SIL members had planted over the years were blooming, along with several varieties of orchids, adding color to the otherwise gold and green foliage. From where he stood he could see the horseshoe-shaped curve of the lake as it bent around a mass of jungle, and he was amazed at how much larger the lake actually was compared to the small tip he could see from his house.

26

Suddenly a loud roar sustained over several seconds pierced the stillness. Ray recognized the sound and took a pair of glasses out of his shirt pocket and adjusted them over his nose. He searched the edge of the jungle that surrounded the lake looking for the bright red fur of the howler monkey that had emitted the noise. After a quick scan he gave up and put his glasses back into his pocket. The monkey must be too deep in the woods to be seen.

Arriving at the farmhouse, Ray joined his friends huddled under a tree to escape the hot sun. Vincent's family consisted of a handful of adults and several children who were busy chasing the chickens and ducks in the yard. A pig lay in the shade of the house, its pink ears twitching at the flies that flew around its head. Once it got up and headed toward the open doorway of the house, but a spotted mutt who sat guarding the door drove it back to its sheltered corner. The women, who had been stirring their aluminum pots when Ray walked up, began ladling out the lunch—yuca, boiled potatoes and rice, and a piece of tough meat. The hungry guests welcomed the meal and everyone enjoyed the company.

At two o'clock Ray returned home to find Doris lying sideways across the armrests of a big porch chair, an iced drink by her side and a book in her hands. "Have a nice visit?" she asked her husband as he walked up.

"Real nice. Hot though."

"Are you still going into town?"

"For a short bit. Sure you don't want to come?"

Doris looked over the top edge of her tortoiseshell-framed glasses at Ray and smiled.

"No, I guess not. I won't be gone long." Ray bent over his wife and kissed the top of her head.

"Don't forget the potluck," she reminded him.

"I'll be back before dark," he responded.

27

Ray took off on his Suzuki DR-250 motorcycle toward Puerto Lleras, a small riverside town about four miles away. Riding along the dusty trails, he thought about the security situation. For the past several weeks the *llanos* had been filled with more violence than usual, and a ban had been initiated prohibiting any SIL member from traveling into or out of the center alone. Just the day before, however, he had met with George Kavanaugh and Ed Mann to determine what measures to take now that the local elections were over, which hopefully meant the violence would subside. Previous to the meeting he had spoken with the local authorities and asked if it was okay for "us *gringos*" to come into town. "No problem. Everything is under control. That's what we're here for," was the response. So it was decided in that meeting to relax the restrictions a little and allow the Lomalinda residents to travel into Puerto Lleras alone if they desired.

Although it couldn't be helped, Ray felt bad it had been so long since his last visit into town and was anxious to see his friends again, especially the little ones. These children, innocent casualties of the terrible poverty and violence that permeated the countryside, were too young to understand why their friend had stayed away.

As he neared town, Ray slowed the motorcycle and took in the scene at the plaza before him. People, young and old, were sitting or standing under whatever shade they could find, sipping cold drinks and wiping the sweat from their faces. Too far away to hear their conversations, he knew what they were talking about—how low the river was, how hot the day was, when the rains would return.

Standing in the shade of a pickup truck but in plain view, two prostitutes flirted with a man. On the opposite side of the street, several kids sat in the dirt—barefoot and in tattered clothes—playing a game. Ray did not know all the children by name but was aware that a handful of them were homeless. In this country where legalized prostitution allowed women to sell their bodies in order to make a living, these unwanted ones always emerged the victims.

Jesus said that it is not the well who need the doctor but the sick. Surely here is spiritual sickness, Ray thought, looking over the dozens of people before him and pondering the lives they represented. Spiritual sickness that manifested itself in many physical ways. Once, he had asked a local lab technician what disease was treated most often at the hospital where he worked. The answer rolled off the technician's tongue without a second thought: venereal disease.

As he parked his bike in front of a local electronics shop, Ray nodded a greeting at a few people he knew. A couple stared at him, their looks sending shivers down his spine. The others looked away. *Have I done something?* he wondered. He took off his sunglasses and entered the shop.

"Ramón! Where have you been?" Hermán, the man behind the counter, extended his hand toward Ray. Ray shook it.

"Busy! How's business here?"

"I always have work, but the people don't have the money to pay for the repairs."

Ray nodded. From behind him he heard the footsteps of another man entering the shop. Seeing Ray he quickly turned around to leave, but Ray caught sight of him.

"Héctor, a blessed *Semana Santa* to you," Ray said, holding out his hand.

Héctor, a stout man in his mid-forties with a long, bushy moustache that hid his mouth, looked awkwardly at Ray's hand in midair. Instead of shaking it he shoved his hand into his pocket. He grunted out something that resembled Ray's name, then looked at Hermán. "I need to talk to you, but it can wait," he said, then hurried out.

Ray cocked his head in bewilderment but said nothing. After visiting with Hermán for a few more minutes, he left for the local government office to say hello to a few officials he knew. On the way he approached some young people on a four-wheel trailer being pulled behind a tractor. Dressed in costume, they looked as though they were part of a parade. Ray stopped and said hello. As they were talking, three young girls, sisters, ran up: Isabela, age twelve; Lady, eight; and Gilma, five.

"Don Ramón, are you coming to visit our house?" the girls pleaded, grabbing Ray's hands and dancing around in the street.

"I guess I have an invitation to attend to," Ray said to the group of teenagers. "Have fun!"

Dragging their friend along by his arms, the three girls pulled Ray the short distance to their modest home, where two little boys ran up to greet him. Their father, Mañuel, was a fisherman and an honest, hardworking man. Occasionally, when the river ran low and the fishing became difficult, Lomalinda would loan him some money, interest free, from their benevolence fund. But he always paid it back, and it was evident from the good shape of his house and health of his family that he used the money wisely. Seeing Ray nearly engulfed in a sea of waving arms and jumping feet, Mañuel shooed the children off to fetch a drink for their guest from their small refrigerator.

After visiting for a while with Mañuel, Ray asked the kids if they wanted a ride on the back of his bike before he left. The boys declined and disappeared, but the girls shrieked in delight and began scrambling aboard. With Gilma sitting in front of Ray and Lady behind him on the seat, Isabela sat on the rack secured over the back tire. Ray drove slowly with his precious cargo, heading out of town about three miles, and stopped briefly at the *finca* (farm) of a friend who worked in the mayor's office before returning the girls to their home.

From there he drove to the house of another young friend, Neli, a precocious twelve-year-old, and her mother, Melba, on the outskirts of town. Neli never knew her father. Melba sold lottery tickets for a living, a burgeoning enterprise in the smaller towns and big business in the larger cities.[1] Ray felt sorry for the poverty-stricken people who got sucked into spending what little money they earned on the lottery—winning was a dream that would never come true for most of them.

Driving up to Melba's front door, Ray remembered the first time he met Neli at an awards ceremony at one of the local primary schools. The ceremony was well attended, and soon there were no seats left to accommodate the crowds who kept coming in. When Neli and her mother arrived they walked up and stood next to Ray, who had come early enough to find a seat. Suddenly Neli plopped herself onto Ray's knee. What a surprise! Later, after learning her father had disappeared before she was born, Ray knew God had honored him by allowing him to be a father figure to the fatherless.

Hearing the bike approach, Neli came to the doorway. A big smile broke across her face. "Mama, it's Don Ramón!" she cried, then ran out and greeted Ray with the customary kiss on the cheek.

Ray patted the seat of the motorcycle. "Want to go for a ride?" he asked. Ray helped Neli onto the seat, and together they pulled away from the house.

"I have to go to *Finca Bonaire* to measure something; do you want to go?"[2] Ray asked. The girl nodded in reply. The underground electrical line that ran across the swamp from the road to the *finca* had burned out, so he wanted to measure the distance with his motorcycle odometer in order to get an estimate for a new line.

When they arrived at the *finca,* Ray noticed some young adults standing around by the front gate, which exited onto the main road. There was a water faucet by the gate so it wasn't unusual for people from Puerto Lleras to come and fill their buckets with clean water, but these youths did not have buckets and seemed uninterested in the faucet. They appeared to be waiting for someone.

Ray greeted the group as he passed. They responded cordially but would not look him in the eye. Again, an uncomfortable feeling swept over him. After taking the measurements he needed, Ray took Neli home.

"Do you and your mom want to go to church tomorrow? It's Good Friday, you know," Ray asked the girl as she lifted her leg over the bike seat to dismount.

"*Sí*, we would like that. What time?"

"I'll pick you up a little before noon." Ray turned his bike around and waved to Neli and Melba, now standing in the doorway. He looked at his watch. Five-thirty. He had time for one or two more visits.

Benny, age five, was one of nine children who lived with their widowed mother in town. A fire early in Benny's life had left severe scars on his face, arms, and hands, and Ray had facilitated surgical help for the boy. The year before, he had taken Benny to Bogotá, where they were met by a courier of Healing the Children of Michigan. Benny spent four months in Grand Rapids, where he underwent three surgeries to remove scar tissue that had restricted his mobility. Now he was back home.

When Ray arrived at Benny's house, his mother was not home, and Melena, Benny's eleven-year-old sister, was taking care of the children. Ray stayed for a couple minutes and visited with them, daydreaming about the times they had stopped at the local ice cream parlor and wishing they were all eating a dish of soft ice cream that very minute!

From there Ray headed for home, stopping at one more neighborhood along the way—*Barrio Popular*. There an elderly woman, Olga, lived with her three grandchildren while her unmarried daughter worked at a *finca* a couple hours away, making thirty dollars a month. Olga was not in good health and struggled to care for the three active children. With only her daughter's income she could not afford shoes and books to send the children to school, so through Lomalinda's benevolence fund, Ray provided the necessary supplies for the children to attend the local public school. Only the year before, Olga and the children had been living in a tar paper shack on the outskirts of town. But a few months ago, a group of young people from the United States—hearing of Olga's plight and raising the funds themselves—had come and built her the brick house in which she now lived.

Ray visited with Olga and the children for several minutes, then, looking at his watch, wished them a blessed *Semana Santa.* It was 6:15, and if he didn't hurry, he would be late for the potluck.

As the sun disappeared below the horizon, Ray sped along the dirt roads leading toward the back gate into Lomalinda. Hordes of bugs appeared with the darkening sky, so he stopped and pulled a pair of glasses out of a denim shoulder bag and put them on. As he drove along he passed several groups of people walking and riding bicycles. Probably heading to church, he thought. He recognized a couple of the families and said hello; they returned his greeting with awkward glances and hushed whispers. Baffled by their response, he waved at some of the children—a few of whom had been deserted by one parent or both parents and were living with a relative—and wondered what it was like growing up in a world where one felt unwanted. He thanked God for his own loving parents and for the opportunity he had to share a caring God with these little ones.

Ray continued on down the road that took him back to *Finca Bonaire.* In the field to his right a herd of brahma bulls grazed, their lustrous white coats and pigmented horns losing color in the dusk of the evening. With his glasses still on as he approached the back gate to the center, he hardly noticed the Colombian man walking along the side of the road headed in the same direction. He idled the Suzuki up to the gate and began to unlock it.

Suddenly the Colombian, who by now had caught up with him, drew a gun from his jacket. Ray froze in place, his hand still holding the lock. Just then two other Colombians ran out from the surrounding trees, guns drawn and aimed at Ray's head.

"What do you want?" Ray asked.

No response. The three men edged closer.

"I don't have much money . . ."

"Get off your bike and come with us!" the man closest to him barked. "Someone wants to talk to you."

Ray reached over and turned the ignition off, leaving the key dangling in the bike. He hadn't completely dismounted his motorcycle when the man closest to him ripped the denim bag off his shoulder and snatched the radio from his belt. The man threw the radio into the bag.

"*Vamos!* Let's get out of here!" he said in his native Spanish. He pushed Ray across the path and through the grass field on the other side. Suddenly, hearing a staticky noise emitting from the denim bag, they stopped. *He tripped the radio,* Ray thought. *I wonder if Doris is listening.* The man holding the bag opened it up and shut the radio off. They took off again.

With the point of a gun within inches of his back, Ray was forced up the side of a hill, through a gate, and toward the house of one of the families he had passed on the road. No wonder they wouldn't look at him and everyone had acted so strangely that day! There are few secrets in Colombia, and sometimes it's hard to know who your friends are.

They ran past the house and through the field on the other side of the hill and kept running until they came to a jungle-lined stream. Realizing their intention to cross over, Ray objected: "I can't swim!"

Pointing to a dugout canoe waiting along the shore, the leader said, "You won't have to. Get in."

The three men climbed in behind the captive. As Ray lay facedown in the bottom of the canoe, they pushed off from shore. Feeling the boat rock back and forth and the force of the water against the wood beneath him made Ray's stomach turn, and he fidgeted in his discomfort. He had been in plenty of boats before, but never one so small and low to the water. To his relief, they reached the other side in a few minutes and got out. Again he was forced to run and keep pace with his three young captors. As they approached a field of banana trees, his side began to cramp up and he felt as though his legs would collapse beneath him. Suddenly he stopped and bent over.

The men, who had relaxed their hold on their weapons, once again pointed their pistols at Ray and flipped off the safety latch.

"Keep moving or I'll kill you!" one of them sneered.

Bent over and huffing exaggeratedly, Ray waved a finger at the man. "You don't understand . . . I've got a bad heart . . . I can't keep up this pace." This was not the truth, but he knew he was reaching his limit and had to slow the guerrillas down.

The three men looked at each other, speaking in Spanish so fast Ray couldn't understand them, then began taking turns pulling and pushing the captive along. They ran along like this for several miles, through fields of dry rice that looked like onion tops. Every once in a while Ray looked over his shoulder. In the grayish white layer of fog hovering among the treetops he could see the lights of Puerto Lleras and Lomalinda reflecting from the valley below and twinkling like stars in the night sky.

35

They kept running until they reached a yellow, two-room cement schoolhouse. Ray had been there less than a month before, digging a well for the school's use. They passed the school and approached a house on the other side.

"Don't say a word . . . don't even make a sound!" Ray's kidnappers warned.

They crept past the house as quietly as they could, then went down a steep grade on its far side to a wooden footbridge that stretched across a small gorge. Ray had been here, too, and took comfort in seeing these familiar landmarks. They crossed over the bridge and went down the hill on the other side to the banks of the wide Ariari River. They walked along the stony river bank about a mile until they came upon another dugout canoe, this one larger than the first.

Here we go again, thought Ray. In the moonlight the river looked very wide at that spot, several hundred feet, and though the weather was only now transitioning to the rainy season, the water ran swiftly downstream. Looking at the canoe bobbing up and down with the lapping current made Ray nervous.

"Get in!" one of the men said with a shove.

As before, Ray lay facedown in the bottom of the canoe. This time he remained perfectly still, not wanting any extraneous movement to upset the boat. On the other side of the river, he and his captors crawled on all fours up the steep bank and crept up to another farmhouse. There they found a horse, saddled up and tied to a post. Ray mounted the horse as the three men conferred quietly together. With one of the men holding the reins of the horse, they entered the woods. Suddenly one man dashed ahead on foot and disappeared. Within a couple miles, the one taking up the rear was nowhere to be found; somewhere along the way he'd gotten lost. That left just one man, who had the horse by the reins and was leading it on foot through the thick underbrush. *Good. At least now we're one against one,* Ray thought, wondering how he might get away without being shot.

Suddenly some branches snapped up ahead. The man leading the horse halted, waiting to see who was approaching. Finally, two boys broke through a thicket of trees and stopped in their tracks. The terrified look on their faces told Ray they weren't expecting to find anyone else on the trail.

"I think you want to be going *this* way," Ray's captor ordered, taking the boys by the shoulders and forcibly turning them in another direction. Immediately the boys burst into a run. "And I don't want to see you again!" the man yelled after them.

Ray and his kidnapper went on for another half hour until they came to a well-maintained road. Along the side of the road lay a cement power pole. The man told Ray to dismount and take a seat on the pole. The captive obliged, happy to be off the horse's back. He could tell from the way his jeans felt against the skin on the inside of his legs that he had saddle sores.

They waited almost an hour. Eventually two headlights appeared as a sports utility vehicle rumbled up the gravel road. The man, who had kept the barrel of his revolver pointed at Ray the entire time, told him to stand up.

Before the car had a chance to come to a complete stop, the back doors flew open and two other men hopped out. One took Ray by the shoulders and held him tight while the other tied a blindfold at the back of his head. "Get into the car!" the man standing in front of him said. Bending over and feeling his way into the vehicle, Ray could sense the man's hot breath on his face and wondered if he would ever see his family again.

The Crisis Committee

March 31 to April 1994

Doris Rising stood at her kitchen sink and rinsed the few dishes she had dirtied preparing for a radio department potluck that evening. Expecting to hear word from Ray that he was on his way home from Puerto Lleras, she crossed the living room and entered the radio room, where a two-way radio sat on a table in the corner. She turned it on. Silence. As she pivoted toward the kitchen, a sudden noise drew her back. She leaned closer to the radio and listened, trying to make sense of the commotion she heard: scuffling feet followed by heavy breathing. Most likely Ray had offered some of the poor children rides on his motorcycle. Had he fallen off his bike? she wondered.

After listening in disbelief to a minute of confusing noises mingled with more hard breathing, Doris thought she heard muffled voices: "*Vamos!* Let's get out of here . . ." Suddenly she flinched as the radio went dead. Her imagination running wild in a region of the world where kidnappings are commonplace, she pictured Ray being dragged off his bike and didn't want to believe it. She stared at the radio momentarily, waiting, hoping to hear her husband come on and explain what had happened. Dead silence. Something's wrong!

She got on the phone and called Ed Mann, head of security at Lomalinda, telling him what had just happened. Ed and Jim Fleming, also on the security team, immediately went out to search the property and surrounding area for Ray. Within minutes they found his Suzuki DR-250 motor-cycle—keys still in the ignition—and a piece of his denim shoulder bag several feet from the back gate where the path to Lomalinda met with another road. Shrouded in darkness, Ed and Jim hollered Ray's name into the night, hoping for a response. Nothing. They searched up and down the dirt road a short distance with their flashlights.

Sensing foul play, Ed suddenly yelled out, "Jim! Turn off your flashlight!"

"Okay . . . why?" Jim responded. Both flashlights went off, and Ed approached Jim in the darkness.

"Because they may still be out there," Ed whispered. An eerie feeling passed over Jim. He hadn't thought of that possibility. Unclipping a radio from his belt, Jim radioed their suspicions back to his house, where his wife, Karen, manned the radio. From the radio room in her home, Doris listened in on the conversation.

"Karen, this is Jim. Do you copy? Over."

"I'm here; go ahead," Karen replied.

"We found his bike back by the rear gate. The keys are still in the ignition and there's a piece of that denim shoulder bag he carries lying on the ground. I don't like the looks of this. Over."

With a heavy heart, Doris took her casserole and went to the potluck to be in the company of her friends and await news. After returning to the center, Ed phoned George Kavanaugh, acting director of SIL's work in Colombia while Brian Gray was out of the country. Listening carefully to every detail Ed conveyed, George concurred: It looked as though Ray had been abducted. Reluctantly George went to the home where the potluck was underway and relayed everything to Doris and the others. The kidnappers had left no communication saying who they were, and there was no way of knowing when they would try to make contact. But George guessed they would eventually; the SIL staff had to be prepared for when that time came. Joining hands around the dinner table, the group prayed for Ray's safety and for wisdom to know how to handle the situation.

George spent the next forty-eight hours notifying Colombian and U.S. authorities of the abduction, as well as officials within the Wycliffe and SIL organizations. He assembled a group of crisis committee members to handle communications with the various agencies that would need to be contacted—government, human rights, and other organizations—as well as deal with the press, and, of utmost importance, prepare for negotiations, assuming Ray's captors would eventually make their demands known.[3]

After being told that contact from the kidnappers might be a long time coming and their presence might endanger any negotiations, Doris, Rollin, and Ray Jr., who arrived from Bogotá where he was working at the time, packed up their belongings in anticipation of returning to the States.[4] With only five weeks left until high school graduation with his classmates in Lomalinda, Rollin was especially reticent about leaving.

Meanwhile, the other several dozen families at Lomalinda tried to carry on with their daily activities, but an undercurrent of uncertainty prevailed in the center. What would happen to Ray, to Doris, and the boys? What would happen to Lomalinda?

Alone and Unsettled

April 1994

Shortly before Doris left Colombia for the States, she packed two waterproof bags for her husband, which were sent via two separate couriers in hopes that at least one of them would reach Ray. Combined, they contained a red pocket NIV New Testament in English with Ray's name written on the inside cover, clothing, his rain poncho, toilette articles, and medicine.

On April 11, Doris and her two sons flew to Minneapolis, leaving her life of over two decades—and her husband—nearly fifteen hundred miles behind. For two weeks she visited with her family and Ray's mother in Minnesota, then proceeded to Waxhaw, North Carolina (home of JAARS), where their house had been leased out. There, on her own for the first time in nearly thirty years, she set up housekeeping, reestablished contacts, and learned to keep busy while waiting for news of Ray.

Without her husband's presence, the days seemed long and unsettled for Doris. Old habits, no matter how pleasant or irritable, grind a pattern of comfort into life; when these patterns are broken, life is disrupted until a new routine can be found. When Ray disappeared, Doris's life was changed in an instant—her sleeping patterns and feelings of security, her time schedule, even her sense of worth, as she no longer had a partner to lovingly prepare meals for or hold conversations with. It was almost as though she'd suffered a death in her husband's loss, but she could not truly "move on." She was trapped in a limbo of uncertainty over which she had no control.

Day after day, her heart and soul beckoned her to action: *Do something to get your husband back!* But in that still, small voice that comes with persistent prayer, God spoke: "Be still, and know that I am God."

We don't often consider that sometimes Jesus is our strength simply to sit still. "Be still, and know that I am God" (Psalm 46:10). Our natural tendency when we have a painful happening in our lives is to go into action—do something. Sometimes it is wiser to sit and just be still. The answers will come.[5]

2

The Calling

April to July 1994

> On Call: The kind of work God usually calls you to is the kind of work that (a) you need most to do, and (b) the world most needs to have done. The place God calls you to is the place where your deep gladness and the world's deep hunger meet.
>
> Frederick Buechner

After riding in the car for quite a while with a blindfold over his eyes, Ray and his abductors finally came to a halt along a deserted road. One of the men removed the blindfold, then instructed Ray to get out of the car. After a short conversation with the driver, he and two others led the hostage down a long grassy slope and into a little house made of wooden planks. "Try to get some rest," the man said, pointing to a bed covered with mosquito netting in a small room.

Ray's feet were swollen and his leather cowboy boots would not come off, so he asked his abductors to help him.

Sitting on the bed, Ray held out one leg, then the other, as one of the kidnappers yanked on the boots until they finally slid off the captive's hurting feet. Then the guerrillas left the room. Ray heard them outside discussing who would stand guard and what hours they would change off, then he fell into an unsettled sleep.

After three hours they woke Ray up and told him to put his boots back on. They headed back up the hill toward the road, where a four-wheel-drive SUV was waiting. After a short trip, they came to a tree that had fallen across the road.

"Get out and start walking," the driver announced.

Ray and the others began down the road. As they walked, the sky began to brighten on the horizon. Soon the sun would be up. After a couple hundred yards, a man appeared, short and plump, with very dark skin and a straw hat. Presuming him to be a leader of some sort, Ray kept walking as the man sidled up to his side.

"I understand you have some heart problems. Is that true, or is it just because you're *gordo*?"

"It's because I'm out of shape."

"This won't take very long."

Ray remained silent.

"Did you hear about the two French nationals who were just released?"

"Yes, I heard about it on TV," Ray responded.

After walking a short distance, one of the kidnappers took Ray's wristwatch and blindfolded him again. Ray could see beneath his blindfold enough to watch his step, but not straight ahead. After walking a distance, they came to a bridge made of bamboo poles tied together with a handrail on either side. Taking hold of the handrails, Ray shuffled slowly across the bridge, then was led to a small stream. At the water's edge, he got into a dugout canoe.

"Can you swim?" the plump man asked as the canoe began skimming the water.

"No, not even a little bit," the hostage replied in a shaky voice.

After crossing the stream, Ray and his abductors sat on another felled tree, where the blindfold was removed from Ray's eyes. At eight o'clock, eight others arrived. Unlike the group of abductors and the three men at the gate (who were dressed in street clothes), this group was clothed in heavy, solid green pants and long-sleeved shirts, with metal artillery belts draped across their chests and around their waists. Each had a Galil[1] slung over one shoulder. One of them approached the captive.

"Have you ever had any experience in the jungle?"

"Only a little bit, traveling with some Indians several years ago."

"Follow me," the man said, walking away from the stream. A handful of the guerrillas fell in line before the captive, while the rest followed after, leaving the three abductors behind.

As they strode along in silence, occasionally the company in front of Ray turned around to look at their hostage. As they did so Ray noted their faces and was shocked at what he saw: Though each one looked calloused and menacing, some of them appeared to be in their teens—incredibly young to be the cold-blooded killers guerrillas were known to be. A couple of the shorter ones had long hair . . . girls! Ray had heard that the guerrillas recruited females but had hardly believed it. Such a life was rough for the toughest of men, let alone their female counterparts.

As Ray walked in line with the others, the surreal scene around him slowly began transforming into reality. This was not just a bad dream from which he would eventually awaken; he truly was walking in the midst of a guerrilla unit, headed far away from home and civilization as he knew it.

His stomach knotted up and made a noise, whether from hunger or nerves Ray could not tell. The air was warm, but his skin broke out in a cold sweat, and every little breeze sent a fresh shockwave of goose bumps over it. In the distance ahead of them a line of trees thickened into blackness. *A dense jungle,* Ray thought. Assuming his captors had taken him west of Lomalinda and deeper into guerrilla territory, he knew this jungle stretched for miles and grew denser and taller than the one surrounding the lake back home.

Within minutes they reached the line of trees and plunged in. Whereas the guerrillas were used to the thick foliage at their feet and walked quickly onward, Ray tripped and stumbled his way along the path they followed. Each time he fell, the man behind him silently yanked him up by the armpits and thrust him forward with a jerk. Passing quickly under low-hanging boughs and over bare roots and vines, Ray wondered how many snakes he was passing along the way. He hated snakes! Frequently he had to force his way through twisted branches, whose sharp thorns felt like bites from the big red mosquitoes common to the area as they punctured holes in his clothing and pricked his skin. As they pressed forward, Ray's imagination ran wild with visions of branches moving in slitherlike fashion.

After what seemed like hours of stumbling along, they neared a clearing where a noise brought them to a halt. It sounded only like a small animal foraging through the underbrush; still they moved forward cautiously, not wanting to be caught by surprise by someone on the trail. As the path broke into the clearing, they saw the source of the noise—a long line of leaf-cutter ants making their way across the glade. As the insects moved forward, the guard ants in the front row used their long scissorlike pinchers to cut through anything standing in their way. Pressing forward, the trail of ants ate a clean path five inches across through the undergrowth, leaving nothing but dirt behind them.

"Take a wide step as you walk over them," the guerrilla behind Ray said. "They stick to your legs and will bite through your clothes." Ray did as he was told. He did not want to find out if the ants could eat through human flesh as well.

Entering the jungle again on the other side of the clearing, he heard a pack of little titi monkeys as they sat high overhead cracking seed pods open and eating the fruit inside. Here and there he saw an empty pod dropping to the earth. Further on, he heard the occasional piercing screech of a howler monkey high in the treetops. He'd heard them before in Lomalinda, but as they are very elusive creatures he'd never seen one close up.

Stumbling onward, Ray listened to the sounds all around him—shrieks and chirps and rattles and roars—which were both intriguing and frightening. Suddenly the harsh scream of another howler monkey filled the air, causing the hostage to jump. He spun around to see a brown, three-foot-tall monkey with a pouch at its throat vault from a squatting position into a nearby tree and disappear.

In this way the morning passed. As the sun rose in the sky, his surroundings turned into an effervescent sea of every shade of green imaginable. From the leaves of the hundred-foot-tall trees to the fronds of the low-growing ferns to the thick wooded undergrowth, everything was green, even the infrequent banana groves they passed, as well as the bark and thorns of the unusual-looking chonta palms with their gnarly root system.

By looking at the course of the sunrise, Ray determined which direction they had been heading—southwest—into territory few *gringos* had ever traveled. Just as he thought his legs would buckle beneath him, he and his captors broke into another glade where the man in charge called everyone to a halt. He barked out orders to the others, then pointed at Ray and told him to sit down. Understanding the man's gestures more than his words, Ray obeyed. His Spanish had been adequate for Lomalinda, but clearly he would need to work hard at improving his ability to speak and understand his captors.

From his seat on a tree stump, a guard hovering over his head, he watched in amazement for the rest of the day as his captors took the surrounding raw materials—sticks and branches from the smaller trees mingled in with the hundred-foot giants—and turned them into beds, tables, and cabinetry. By the end of the day, the clearing, situated near a stream, had been transformed into a camp.

The "kitchen" was set up beside the river. A rusty fifty-five-gallon drum functioned as a stove, with a tarp above to keep the rain from putting out the fire on the makeshift burners. A large, high table with a tarp for a roof was built as storage for the food. Overhanging the river the guerrillas built a platform for bathing, and near the trail between the kitchen and the rest of the camp they constructed a picnic table and benches. From there the trail led uphill through a cluster of trees to another small clearing, where *caletas*² were built. Nearby was a private area used as a latrine, complete with sanitation holes and green toilet paper. Years of jungle living had certainly taught the guerrillas to be handy.

Evening approached and dinner was prepared. Ray had not had anything to eat since the lunch he'd had at noontime the day before, and with all the recent activity and little sleep, he felt light-headed and famished. Just before the meal was set on the table, the guerrilla leader approached him. Middle-aged, short, and pudgy, he had thin hair and a long, straggly mustache, which hung below his chin.

"So, how are you doing?" the man asked.

"I've been better."

"You have nothing to fear; we don't kill prisoners."

"So what are you holding me for if you don't plan to kill me?"

"We just want to talk to you, that's all. If all goes well you'll be back home in a week. My name is Arnoldo. I'm the commandant. Is there anything you need right now?"

"Well, some toiletries would be nice . . . a Bible, and a notebook to do some writing."

"I'll see what I can do," Arnoldo said. "One more thing, you are not to talk to any of your guards unless responding to an order. Otherwise, there will be trouble!"

For the next week Ray settled into jungle life as best he could, sleeping at night and spending his days on his bed of sticks and chonta palm leaves, washing his clothes and bathing in the cold stream, and trying to stay cool in the hundred-degree heat without the convenience of an electric fan. Meals consisted of tortillas, rice and beans, and occasionally some wild game. No one came to interrogate him, and aside from Arnoldo, the only guerrilla who spoke to him was Ernesto. Like many Colombians, Ernesto had an innate strain of human sentiment that sympathized with the underdog or the unfortunate, and he pitied Ray. Whenever the commandant was out of sight, he stole moments to chat with the captive.

Ray's second week of captivity began with Arnoldo delivering a notebook and pen, along with a small green New Testament written in Spanish with selected psalms in the back. Each day, as Ray spent time in meditation and prayer, he jotted down his thoughts. On April 11, he wrote his first letter to Doris and gave it to the guerrillas, hoping it would be delivered.

After three weeks of clandestine visits between Ernesto and the hostage, Ernesto was squatting beside Ray's *caleta* when the commandant unexpectedly strode by. Seeing the guerrilla talking to the captive, he stopped short.

"Ernesto, what are you doing there?"

Startled, Ernesto jumped to attention. "I . . . I . . . I was just checking on Ramón."

"You know the rules: No one is to speak to the hostage!"

"You're right. I'm sorry. I won't let it happen again," Ernesto said.

The other guerrillas snickered, and Arnoldo took note of their response. Within a week, Ernesto was changed out of camp with a letter of reprimand for befriending the captive. Ray wondered what would happen to him. As the guerrilla walked sullenly from camp, Arnoldo threatened, "Anyone else wishing to consort with the hostage can expect the same!"

Even after the warning, however, out of earshot of the commandant, the other guerrillas asked Ray random questions about his organization, his personal work at Lomalinda, and the facility itself. Ray thought it strange they would risk Arnoldo's wrath just to satisfy their curiosity, but he answered their questions nonetheless. On one occasion, after Ray had washed his clothes in the stream, one of the girls—a fair-skinned nineteen-year-old named Maria—led him into the *llanos* to set his clothes out to dry. Ray had observed Maria over the past few weeks and sensed she was nervous about her assignment and unsure of herself. Most of the time she walked about camp in a fit of bad temper, except when she was near her boyfriend, Adam. At his side, she cooed and did as she was told.

So as not to be seen from the air, Ray put on a green cap to cover his now graying hair, then crept into the tall grass with Maria at his heels. Usually under such circumstances, the guard would sit silently in the grass and ignore the hostage. But this time, after sitting in the grass for nearly an hour, she, too, posed a question of Ray.

"Are there American troops in Lomalinda?"

"No, Lomalinda is a facility where civilians live and work at translating the Bible into indigenous languages. There's no military there."

"Oh, yes there is! We've seen them!"

"Who's seen military troops in Lomalinda? You?"

"Well, no, but I've heard others talk about it . . ."

"Well, whatever they saw, it wasn't the American military. We wouldn't do something stupid like that!"

Suddenly Ray saw Arnoldo standing at the edge of the grass, waving an arm at Maria. "Okay, you can bring him back to camp now." Ray stared at Maria. He had been duped! The indiscriminate questions had been planned all along.

Even with the Bible and notebook, boredom and loneliness beset Ray, and the days passed slowly. Then on April 29, the monotony broke as a couple of military aircraft flew overhead, dropping bombs in the woods near their camp.

"Ramón, those planes are coming from Lomalinda!" Maria screamed, ducking into her *caleta* and gathering her things.

Not knowing what to do, Ray crouched under his shelter. "That's ridiculous!" he yelled back. "I told you there are no military troops at Lomalinda!"

With the ground shaking beneath them and the sky filling with dirt and smoke, the camp burst into a frenzy of activity as the guerrillas darted every which way for their belongings.

"Ramón, quick!" Arnoldo yelled at the captive as he skirted past his *caleta* and into the surrounding woods, followed by the others.

Ray shoved his belongings into his backpack and bolted out of camp after the others. As he ran through the woods, the thought flashed through his mind that if he could find a clearing, maybe the military would spot him and he might have the opportunity to identify himself as a kidnapped

American. But just as quickly as the idea came to him, he dismissed it. Dressed now in a guerrilla uniform, the military soldiers would likely shoot first and ask questions later! As he ran, his head filled with thoughts not his own: *Don't be like Moses, who took matters into his own hands, killed the Egyptian, then suffered repercussions because of it. I have a better plan, including some things for you to learn along the way.*

The guerrillas and Ray ran hard for nearly an hour, leaving the explosions behind them. Finally they slowed to a halt. Arnoldo ordered everyone to relax as he radioed in to check on the military maneuvers. After several minutes, he approached the group.

"Were they after us?" Ray blurted out, wide eyed.

"They were after any encampments in the area; if we'd stayed there, they would have found us," the commandant said. "We're not safe here either, but we'll stay until dark, then move on."

Ray pulled out his Bible and notebook. Suddenly Arnoldo snatched the notebook from his lap. "What are you writing about?"

"I take notes on my devotions, my Bible meditation."

Arnoldo looked at Ray's notations, but as they were in English, he could not read them. "I think I'll just keep this—"

"Oh, no, don't do that!" Ray pleaded.

"I think you're writing about us and planning your escape. If you try anything I'll kill you myself!" Arnoldo scowled at the captive, then walked away.

After that, the entire camp picked up and moved every couple of weeks to avoid detection from the military. Not wanting to leave behind any trace of their existence, before departing from their old site, the guerrillas tore all the furniture apart and strewed the wood around inconspicuously. Lying on his *caleta,* Ray watched in amazement while his captors destroyed everything they had worked so meticulously to build only weeks before.

One morning in May, Ray was reading about wisdom in the first chapter of James when Arnoldo approached his *caleta*. "Time to move, Ramón. Pack up," he said. Each time Ray heard those words he cringed, but as before, he obediently put all his belongings into his backpack and sat on a log awaiting the commandant's order to fall out. Watching the guerrillas as they busily tore apart the camp, he realized no one was watching him. Nonchalantly he strolled up an incline to a stand of small trees, where he pulled a small Buck knife from his pocket and began carving in the tree bark.[3] Slowly the words "Ramón de LmL" took shape on the tree.[4] Just as he finished the last letter, he sensed someone watching him. Whirling around, he saw Adam—an older black man and experienced guerrilla—scrutinizing him from the center of camp. Remembering what he had just read, Ray whispered a quick prayer to God. Should he scrape the initials off the tree? If he did that, surely Adam would suspect he was doing something evasive. If he left them there, he could make up some excuse for doing it, like boredom.

"Ramón!" Adam called, waving at Ray. Ray left the initials and obeyed, walking past the guerrilla to pick up his backpack where he'd left it beside the log. As he did so the guerrilla ran over to the tree and scraped the initials off, then ran up to Arnoldo.

"Don Ramón scraped his initials in one of those trees!" he said, pointing to the little stand of trees on the hill.

"You idiots! Why don't you watch him more closely! He could escape and none of you would know it!" Arnoldo bawled.

The rest of the day the guerrillas treated Ray cruelly, not helping him with his chores or loaning him anything he needed as he set up his things in their new campsite. Later that evening Ray approached one of the girls as she cooked dinner. "I was just playing around with Adam."

"Well, you got us all in trouble."

"I realize that and I'm sorry," Ray said. Soon the guerrilla passed his "excuse" and apology on to the others, who got over their anger. Still, Arnoldo sent two guerrillas back to all their previous campsites, making sure the captive had not left any other traces of his whereabouts.

June arrived, bringing very hot, stale air to the countryside. In the guerrilla camp everyone sat around fanning themselves in a sweltering stupor, too hot to move.

On the seventh of the month, Ray began his daily devotions by reading Psalm 46: "God is our refuge and strength, an ever-present help in trouble. Therefore we will not fear, though the earth give way and the mountains fall into the heart of the sea, though its waters roar and foam and the mountains quake with their surging" (vv. 1–3).

After a couple hours of reading and with the weather too hot to exercise, he joined everyone else in camp by lying in the shade of his *caleta*. In the stillness, he felt a slight tremor shake his shelter. He looked up into the heavens, wondering if bombers were flying overhead, but the sky was clear and silent. The shaking continued, worsening by the second, then ended suddenly with a huge jolt. Earthquake! As the shadows moved back and forth across the floor of the camp, the captive looked up to see the giant trees swaying in the aftermath of the event. Immediately the words of the psalmist came to mind: though the earth give way and the mountains quake, we will not be afraid. As the words sank in, Ray realized God was speaking to him: *You do not need to be afraid, for I am with you.* The Creator of the universe had sent an earthquake to comfort Ray and teach him that nothing is outside of God's control and power.

With this object lesson fresh in his mind, Ray wrote a letter to his wife, telling how the earthquake was God's way of encouraging him to wait patiently for the fulfillment of God's promises.

July brought another move. After several hours of walking with their packs bulging with equipment, the line of captive and guerrillas collapsed along the woody trail. Ray unbuttoned his shirt a ways, fanning himself to cool his sweaty skin and keep the mosquitoes away. Noticing that a handful of them were somewhat separated from Arnoldo and the others, José, a short guerrilla with dark, curly hair and a pock-marked face, leaned toward Ray. "Ramón, do you know any jokes?"

"Well . . ." Ray thought. "There was this Pastuso[5] who wanted to sell his cow to a Paisa for a million *pesos* (about a thousand dollars). One morning the Pastuso said to his mother, 'I'm going to sell the cow to some Paisa today for a million *pesos.*'

"'Well, Son, that's a lot of money for a cow, and how come you're going to sell it to a Paisa for that inflated price?'

"'Well, Mom, you know how the Paisas are, always taking advantage of us.'

"So the Pastuso left with the cow. Later that day he returned to his house. 'Well, Sonny, did you sell the cow to a Paisa for a million *pesos?*'

"'Well, Mom, we agreed on a trade. We now have two chickens worth five hundred thousand *pesos* each!'"

The guerrillas laughed.

After a short rest they were off again. A while later they approached a gorge about thirty feet deep with a river at the bottom and a felled log across its top edge. Ray looked at the gorge and backed away.

"I hope you don't expect me to walk over that."

"What's the matter?" Arnoldo asked.

Ray looked over the edge again. Again he backed away. "I can't swim, and I know looking down into that river will make me nervous and I'll lose my footing. I can't do it!"

Arnoldo scratched his head. Pointing to a few long vines, he instructed the guerrillas to attach them on either side of the log as a handrail. Slowly the captive approached the log and grabbed hold of the vines. He inched forward and then stopped, then inched forward again. The log didn't budge. His courage rising, he began walking slowly across the log. Once he looked down and wavered, one foot rising off the log.

"Don't look down, Ramón! Try to think of something besides the river!"

Ray looked ahead at the guerrillas on the opposite edge of the gorge who were encouraging him onward. Suddenly a verse he'd memorized years before popped into his head. "All the days of the oppressed are wretched, but the cheerful heart has a continual feast" (Prov. 15:15). Keeping his eyes fixed on his captors' faces, he broke out into a robust version of the Colombian national anthem. As his feet reached solid ground, a cheer went up among the guerrillas on both sides of the gorge. While waiting for everyone to cross, José clapped Ray's back. "You always give us something to laugh about!" he said. For the first time in his captivity, Ray felt comfort in their presence.

That evening, with the commandant away for the moment, José sidled up to Ray's *caleta*. José was originally from Puerto Lleras. His brother had been killed in a skirmish with the military there, and José felt very bitter toward them and the government. Once he had tried living the fundamentalist Christian life but couldn't sustain the self-discipline it required. So he joined the guerrilla movement, more for the romantic adventure than anything else. But he understood Ray's faith and occasionally defended him before the other guerrillas who mocked the hostage's beliefs.

"Ramón, the girls don't like me because I'm short and not very good looking," he moaned.

"Well, I've heard you sing before; maybe you should serenade them."

"Do you want to hear a poem I just wrote about AIDS?"

Just then Arnoldo walked up. "Do I need to repeat that you are not to talk to the hostage?" he boomed at the young guerrilla. José slinked away.

A few days later Arnoldo carried a large sack into camp and up to Ray's shelter. Immediately Ray recognized his red New Testament from home and opened up the front cover to see his name marked inside. The sack also included his rain poncho, some toiletries, and medicine.

"I see they sent along some medicine, which reminds me, a medic is coming tomorrow to check on you," Arnoldo said.

The next day the medic arrived. As he walked up to Ray's *caleta,* he reached out and shook the captive's hand. As he did so Ray noticed the plastic band he wore on his right arm with the letters FARC[6] written on it in bold type.

"I'm Victor. How are you?"

"Okay, I guess. My nerves are bad from the extended period of time in captivity."

"I have something that might help with that," Victor said, looking in his case for some tablets. "I hear you're a Christian. Do you believe in heaven?"

"Yes, I do. The Bible says God is preparing a place in heaven for me right now."

With a philosophical look on his face, Victor tapped two tablets out into the palm of his hand. "Everything has a life cycle, like a tree. It grows up and dies, and that's it."

Ray could see where the discussion was headed but was not in a proper emotional state to argue, so he just listened.

"Where was Lazarus those days after he died and before he was resurrected?" Victor prodded.

"Your problem is that you're thinking in terms of time—God isn't bound by the laws of time," Ray responded.

The medic looked thoughtful. "I'll be back to check on you in the morning," he said, and left. Shortly the tablets he'd given Ray, which were supposed to make him feel more comfortable with his surroundings, took effect, making him more nervous than before. When the medic returned the following morning, he found his patient in a highly agitated state.

"Why did they take me? I can't handle this anymore!"

Victor looked off to the side to be sure no one was listening, then said, "You may not have anything to do with it, but your country has been doing lots of things here in Colombia." Then he took out another medication and gave it to the captive, which eased his tension.

After he began to feel better, Ray felt ashamed of his outburst. Looking around at his captors, he considered their dedication to the guerrilla movement. They lived in very primitive conditions for years at a time, putting up with all kinds of insects and snakes; took baths, brushed their teeth, washed dishes and clothes in a stream; slept on beds made of sticks; wore heavy wool uniforms in the hot humid weather; walked for hours in the water and mud; sometimes went without food and sleep; constantly dug holes in the ground for sanitation . . . all with no complaints, little thanks, and no pay.

Thinking of this, Ray sensed the Lord saying to him, *Ray, you also have to be a soldier—take your share of suffering, like Paul told Timothy, and do what I tell you. Be careful what you say and watch your life closely.* He thought about the prophet Daniel, whose enemies watched his life vigilantly, looking for some flaw in his ethics or morality with which to trip him up. Daniel and all the prophets of old were called upon by God to fulfill a very specific task. Was it possible that his abduction was no accident but a calling of God to witness to his captors? With these thoughts swirling about in his head, he fell asleep. In the middle of the night, he awoke with a start. A thick cloud cover masked the moon and stars, and the night looked black as coal. As he lay in bed, an eery sensation swept over Ray that a spiritual battle was raging around him. He shuddered. Suddenly he sensed the Lord's voice saying, *The angel of the LORD encampeth round about them that fear him, and delivereth them* (Ps. 34:7 KJV), and his fear vanished.

The next day, Sunday, Arnoldo asked Ray to repair his radio. In exchange, he allowed the captive to listen to whatever he liked for the afternoon.

"But only this once," Arnoldo said, wagging his finger at Ray.

Hungry for Christian fellowship and to hear the Word of God, Ray scanned the dial for Christian programming but found none. Then an idea came to him. If he could just get an antenna high enough, he was sure to pick up something. He found a copper scouring pad on the food storage table. Unwinding it to its full length of eighty feet, he attached one end to the radio, then tied the other end to a stick and threw it up into the trees. To his delight, he could pick up stations all over the hemisphere! He turned the dial until he found an English-speaking voice, Oral Roberts, speaking about faith from the Book of Hebrews. Again he heard the Lord speaking to him about the faithful men of old who obediently yielded to God's calling in their lives. "Yes, Lord," Ray responded in a whisper, "but all of these people had something specific you wanted them to do. What do you want me to do?" He looked down at the little red New Testament in his lap, where the answer leaped out at him: "You need to persevere so that when you have done the will of God, you will receive what he has promised" (Heb. 10:36).

At that moment perseverance sounded difficult if not impossible. But in the days ahead, Ray read James 5:11 and other Bible passages about perseverance, realizing that if God had called him to a task, he would also give him the strength to perform it, just as he did for Jeremiah. Suddenly the words of the prophet, which he'd read years before, coursed through his mind: "Before I formed you in the womb I knew you; before you were born I sanctified you; and I ordained you a prophet to the nations" (Jer. 1:5 NKJV).

With his head bowed in prayer, Ray bowed his heart in submission to God's will.

First Contact

June to July 1994

Within a week after Ray's abduction, one particular man, Ricardo (not his real name), approached the crisis committee offering to serve as a courier between them and Ray's captors. He'd had casual dialogues with the guerrillas in the past and knew how ruthless they could be, yet being Ray's friend, he felt compelled to help in whatever way he could. Thus began many months of inconspicuous commuting in and out of the jungle, carrying medicines in his pockets and letters tucked in his shoes.

Two and a half months passed without a word from Ray's captors; no one knew whether Ray was dead or alive. Finally, on June 9, Ricardo returned to Lomalinda carrying news from the kidnappers. He told George Kavanaugh and Brian Gray, who by that time had returned from the States, that the local front of the Revolutionary Armed Forces of Colombia was holding Ray and demanding a huge ransom for his release.

The next communication from the captors, in early July, contained two letters from Ray as proof that they were in fact holding him and that he was still alive. The first one, dated April 11 and addressed to his wife, gave the committee and Doris their first glimpse into Ray's treatment and well-being:

My Love,

A cordial greeting in the name of Jesus Christ. Many nice memories to you! I miss you and Rollin very much. I am fine. The people here are treating me gently. God is with me each moment.

I am suffering with fungus in the same place as before but they are going to buy the medicine I need. Also, my nerves are bothering me.

I hope that Rollin can finish his studies at Lomalinda.

I have Coca-Cola, apple juice, etc., and also three meals a day.

Happy Birthday!

The second letter, addressed to Doris and the family, contained a notation next to the date of June 7: *"carta numero 8,"* or "letter number 8":

Esteemed Love and Family,

A cordial greeting in the name of Jesus Christ. Many kisses and hugs. I miss you very much and think a lot about you and my ILV [Lomalinda] friends. Praying a lot for all. Waiting for the day when we will be able to see each other again. Especially many greetings to the neighbor and his Mrs. I do not have any news about what is happening with him and you all.

Today I was reading Psalm 46:1–3, "Therefore we will not fear, though the earth give way." Today in the afternoon there was an earthquake in the whole country. Here the trees were moving. A manifestation to me that God will keep the promises to me like he was saying. Psalm 37:5–8,[7] etc.

My health is more or less good. I am struggling with fungus in the same [place] but it is controlled. Sometimes my nerves bother me a lot. I am size 31 or 32 instead of 34. I am bathing every day, I have soap and shampoo and every two days I shave. My hair is now grey in color. Please continue to pray for my health. There are people who have colds.

Tell the neighbor to please get a move on.

Give my mother my greetings. I want her to take care of her health, to eat well and not to worry.

I am thinking a lot about our younger son. I don't know if he can study and live with you or what is best. God knows and He will help you with plans. Also, the other son can get another job there where you will be. I remember talking to him at the last, about these things the last time I was with him. God bless you. I am thinking a great deal about Lot when he went to Sodom. God knows.

Many greetings to your parents and to all the in-laws.

Doris, at home in Waxhaw, received copies of the letters by fax from the crisis committee and was relieved to know Ray was alive and being treated mercifully. Knowing kidnapping is a common occurrence in Colombia and that most of the hostages return home safely encouraged her. *The worst is over,* she thought. *He's alive, and hopefully he'll be home soon.*

Negotiations

June to September 1994

That first contact in June of 1994 opened up negotiations for Ray's release, which was an agonizingly slow and tedious process. Establishing and maintaining a link with the captors was not easy, and discussion almost always required a certain risk of exposure for the individual immediately involved. Exposure was dangerous. The guerrillas, who rarely admitted to kidnappings, frowned upon the intermediary who publicized his mission, and the military and auto-defense groups didn't look kindly on anyone who appeared to be collaborating with the guerrillas. Since messages (written and verbal) transmitted by way of a reliable go-between were the primary means for conducting conversations with Ray's captors, reasonably secure channels had to be built before any fruitful dialogue could take place.

Topping the list of priorities for the crisis committee, then, was identifying individuals who might have contact with the guerrillas and who were credible, dependable, honest, and able to maintain a low profile. Initially a number of people offered to help serve as go-betweens. Besides Ricardo, two such people were Chaddy and Russell Stendal,[8] while other contacts developed during the course of the crisis. Wanting to leave all possibilities open, the crisis committee never closed any doors in favor of others, although they followed specific leads as opportunities arose along the way. Throughout Ray's crisis, the committee was ever grateful for these individuals—while they remained physically and emotionally distant from the guerrillas and could filter out their rhetoric and psychological pressure, these couriers took the full brunt of what the guerrillas dished out.

The next task was to build enough confidence between both sides to sustain a dialogue. Throughout the negotiations, respect and courtesy, with firmness, oiled the wheels that kept the process moving. In Colombia, relationships built on trust and respect form the foundation of nearly every successful venture.

Responding to the guerrillas' verbal or written demands formed another time-consuming task, best left to the crisis committee as a whole rather than any particular individual. When a communication came in, the committee analyzed it and crafted a response, taking into consideration each member's thoughts or concerns. All responses began with a cordial greeting—according to Colombian custom—and attempted to find points of cooperation, with the long-range goal being a successful resolution acceptable to both parties.

As the negotiations proceeded, the crisis team learned quickly that one of their biggest challenges would be handling the multitude of people offering assistance in one form or another, from writing letters to distributing flyers to running messages. Some said they knew of Ray's whereabouts, while others claimed to represent the guerrillas themselves, proposing a completely different means for gaining Ray's release. Evaluating the authenticity and sincerity of each contact's assertion was an exhausting chore, requiring a detailed scrutiny into the facts of the claimant. George Kavanaugh and others on the committee hated judging these people's hearts but knew they must attempt to discern people's motives.

But the biggest problem of all was dealing with the reality of the bottom line—neither SIL nor Ray's family could possibly meet the multimillion-dollar ransom demanded for his release. In addition, SIL has a policy of not giving in to such demands. Though this might sound harsh toward the individual being held captive at the time, to pay a ransom might encourage hostage-taking practices elsewhere in the country and around the world, putting other people's lives at risk. Instead, a slow, careful process of exploring other alternatives is the only viable option.

Like any other type of hostage situation, establishing "proof of life" in Ray's case was a key element upon which everything else hinged. Between June and September of 1994, six such proofs of life were received in the form of letters from Ray, five written to Doris and the family and one to a colleague. Each letter was scrutinized in every detail, making sure the tone matched Ray's personality and style and that the handwriting was recognizably his. In his letters, Ray expressed his faith in and commitment to God but also his loneliness and frustration over not being able to see his family. Although his health held up, he was not used to the harsh jungle environment, and captivity was taking its toll on him mentally and emotionally.[9]

Doris also wrote several letters to her husband during this time, whenever there was an opportunity for one to be delivered with a messenger to the guerrillas. At first her letters were written in English, but the guerrillas rejected them. "Write in Spanish," they said. "Letters in English will not be passed on."[10]

At the beginning of the negotiation process there was an air of optimism that Ray would not be held long. Colombia led the world in kidnappings at that time, and still does—nearly every day someone is kidnapped somewhere in the country while someone else is released. But as the days and weeks ticked slowly by, there was a frustrating sense that nothing was happening. The crisis committee wondered if they were doing everything they could or if there was some small detail they had overlooked that would make the difference. Frequently they felt crushed by the urge for haste—they wanted Ray released *now!*

But it was not to be. Not yet. God had another purpose, which they knew nothing about. As suddenly as the negotiations began in June, they abruptly stopped in September of that year. The crisis committee did not know why, but with elections fast approaching—at the end of October—it is possible the guerrillas' attention was diverted to that arena for the time being. The military was also extremely active in the general region during that time, disrupting the guerrillas' activities as they tried a variety of tactics to derail the election process.

If the months of intense activity were wearing, trying to keep up a normal routine day after long day while waiting to hear any word about Ray was worse. The crisis committee put out feelers in the community, contacting everyone who might have some information or be able to help. They contacted government officials, human rights organizations, and private individuals. They drew up strategies to reopen communication with the guerrillas. But none of these plans prompted renewed negotiations.

During those dark months, hundreds of people across Colombia and the world prayed for Ray's safety and release. For the crisis committee, one particular verse of the Bible—Isaiah 50:10—gave peace and hope that God would, in his time, turn the situation around:

> Who among you fears the LORD?
>   and obeys the word of his servant?
> Let him who walks in the dark,
>   who has no light,
> trust in the name of the LORD
>   and rely on his God.

3

Looking Death in the Eye

July to October 1994

> Do not fear those who kill the body but cannot kill the soul. But rather fear Him who is able to destroy both soul and body in hell.
>
> Matthew 10:28 NKJV

After only two weeks in the same campsite, in mid-July Ray and his captors moved to yet another location, overgrown with ferns and other plants but near a sandy beach. While the others busied themselves with cabinet-making, Jorge began clearing the new area with a machete. Suddenly the knife slipped from his fingers and cut a deep gash in his right leg. Ray was resting inside the mosquito netting of his *caleta* when he heard Jorge cry out.

"What happened? Look at your leg!" Ray exclaimed, running over and kneeling beside the guerrilla.

"Get away; it's nothing," Jorge groused.

"What do you mean, nothing? That's a deep cut. I'll go get the commandant."

"No, he'll sanction me," Jorge groaned, holding his leg.

"Sanction you?"

"You know, dig holes or run supplies!" the guerrilla retorted.

"Well, at least put some pressure on it."

Jorge took a cloth and pressed down on the wound, but blood continued to come, soaking the cloth in seconds. He looked around nervously, not wanting the others to notice his dilemma. To his chagrin Leo, a stocky guerrilla with slick black hair, was heading toward them, wondering what all the commotion was about.[1] After a brief conversation with Jorge, the guerrilla began a mystic chant.

In his nearly twenty-five years of working with the Colombian people, Ray had learned that many Colombians—especially those living in the rural countryside—still practiced folk medicine and witchcraft. Ray knew his God was greater than their beliefs and customs, but rather than argue with them, he looked for opportunities to share Christ with them. Here, God was providing one of those opportunities. Realizing this, he was apprehensive—he did not want to unduly anger his captors. As he thought over what to do next, the words of Christ flooded his mind: *Love your enemy . . . and your neighbor as yourself.* Jorge and Leo were both.

After several minutes Jorge lifted the cloth, hoping the bleeding had slowed. Instantly, blood gushed from the wound, strong as ever. Jorge untied his boot and tipped it upside down. A cupful of blood ran out, forming a puddle on the ground.

"I'm getting the commandant," Ray decided, rising to his feet.

"No! I'll be sanctioned!" Jorge argued.

"You'll be dead if you don't stop the bleeding," Ray muttered, then turned and called Arnoldo.

Sizing up the situation, Arnoldo asked, "Did Leo chant over him?"

"Yes," Ray answered.

"And it's still bleeding?" the commandant exclaimed, his eyes wide with amazement. Like Leo, he believed that invoking the spirits of the dead would heal Jorge's leg and was surprised when the chant had no effect.

"He should lie down, raise his leg up," Ray said. Leo nodded, and both men helped Jorge to his *caleta*. Ray sat at the edge of the bed for a couple of hours, pressing on the wound with a string of clean cloths until the bleeding stopped. For several days the guerrillas took turns tending Jorge's leg, exerting pressure if it began to bleed and changing the dressing frequently. Occasionally, when the others were busy, Ray sat on the guerrilla's *caleta* and changed the dressing himself. A couple of times he prayed aloud for the man, hoping to soften his heart. But all he received for his effort was more cursing. "You *gringos* are all alike . . . thinking more highly of yourselves and your own ways! I don't need you!" he ranted. Ray was very glad when the bleeding finally stopped and Jorge was able to get out of bed.

A couple nights later, while guarding Ray, Leo came and sat beside the captive. "Why do you think my chanting didn't help Jorge?"

"There is only one living God who is able to hear our requests and answer them," Ray responded.

"Is that why you pray all the time?"

"Yes, and read my Bible. The Bible is a book about God. The more I know about God the better I'm able to understand who he is and what he wants of me. That helps me know what to pray for, and then I can feel confident God hears my prayers."

A long silence followed Ray's response. Finally, a thoughtful Leo asked, "Ramón, do you think there is salvation for me too?"

"Salvation is for everyone. Leo, the Lord God is waiting for you, like a loving father waiting for his wayward son to come home. Open your heart to him and receive his forgiveness and salvation!" Ray pleaded.

Leo stared at the captive for a moment then walked away.

With the exception of a few isolated incidents such as this one, the guerrillas did not fraternize with their hostage. Months of solitary confinement were taking their toll on Ray, inducing intense loneliness and despair. Every waking moment he spent thinking of his family, and every night he dreamed of escaping his prison or running from military attacks. Slowly, one thought pervaded his mind: Physically and mentally, could he survive? For days on end he prayed for relief with no apparent results, until his birthday, August 2. At sunrise that morning a new commandant strolled into camp, a slender, chestnut-skinned man with a crooked arm. Ray wondered if it had been broken at one time and not set properly. A bush of jet black hair, curly and thick, framed his pockmarked face. After relieving his predecessor and inspecting the unit, he squatted down next to Ray and introduced himself as Omar.

"So, how have they been treating you? Is the food okay?" the new commandant asked.

"The food's okay, but they've kept me in isolation. It sure would help to have someone to talk to," Ray answered, nodding toward the guerrillas.

The commandant raised his eyebrows. "One of the men wrote saying Arnoldo was too harsh on you. Well, that's changed now. You can talk to anybody you want."

With that welcome, Omar looked around at the eight uniformed men and women who were lazing around on their *caletas*. He began barking orders at them, and the guerrillas jumped and snapped into action, digging sanitation holes, preparing food, or cleaning their rifles.

"You were saying?" Omar asked.

"Well . . ." Ray hesitated.

"Go ahead."

"In the evenings everyone gathers around the guard's chair next to the fire. They talk and laugh late into the night and I can't sleep. Is it possible for the guard to *stand* watch instead of sitting in a chair?"

"Anything else?" Omar asked.

"One other thing, I guess. I have a hard time with your man Jorge. He's very crude. Can my *caleta* be moved away from his?"

After a few more questions Omar left Ray alone. Ray wondered if he'd said too much. *Time will tell,* he thought. After Omar left, Jorge walked up to the prisoner and sat down on a log. Always stony-eyed and sneering, Jorge never smiled or laughed except at his own vulgar jokes. Already Ray knew he did not like him.

"So you're lonely, eh? Aw, that's too bad! Well, I'm here to keep you company now; you want my company?"

Ray shrugged.

"You hear from your wife? Oh, that's right, you're not supposed to talk to us," Jorge snorted.

"The commandant just said I could talk to anyone," Ray retorted. "Including you."

Jorge was silent.

"No, I haven't heard from her." Ray forced himself to look Jorge in the eyes. The guerrilla's face was cold and cruel, and it frightened him.

"I bet by now she's forgotten all about you, found herself another man, eh?" Jorge said with a toothy laugh. He turned to face the others, massaging his leg as he did so. (This was not the leg that had just been wounded, but the other one.) "Hey, what do you think, *amigos?* Think his wife still remembers him?" Some of the guerrillas snickered, including Maria. A few weeks before, her boyfriend,

Adam, had been changed out of camp, and she had been bossy and rebellious ever since.

"I've seen you rub your leg before. Does it hurt?" Ray asked, wanting to change the subject.

"Got shot a couple years ago; it never healed right." Jorge pulled up his dark green pant leg to reveal an ugly scar.

"What happened?" Ray asked, frowning at the leg.

"My patrol got ambushed; helicopters came in on all sides loaded with military troops. They were retreating to the chopper when one of them shot me. Medic was killed, so my comrades had to stitch me up themselves."

"Were very many injured?"

"Many casualties, but more of them than us!" Jorge chuckled with a bloodthirsty grin. "You ever kill anybody?" he asked casually, like it was an everyday question.

"No, I'm a man of peace," Ray answered.

"That's too bad," Jorge said dully.

For several minutes Jorge silently eyed Ray as though measuring him up, then headed for his *caleta*. At lunchtime Maria, who had been cooking a vegetable soup, approached the captive with a bowl.

"Here," she said gruffly, setting the bowl on the edge of Ray's *caleta* and brushing her shoulder-length light brown hair away from her sweaty face. She stood there for a moment. "Well, do you need anything else?"

"No . . . yes, come to think of it," Ray answered. "Could you boil me some water? My supply's getting low." Maria tromped off. "Thank you," Ray called after her. He began wondering if wanting to communicate with the guerrillas was such a good idea after all.

Since the beginning of his captivity, Ray and his band of captors had been picking up camp and moving at least once a month. Each time a new campsite had to be selected and prepared, including building new *caletas*, tables, storage cabinets, and sanitation facilities. All of these preparations took about a week. If time permitted, the commandant sent out two or three guerrillas to scout and prepare a new site ahead of time. Frequently, though, with the military on their heels, they moved unexpectedly. Then the guerrillas would shout at Ray to tear down his shelter and pack up his few belongings with breakneck speed. Those times unnerved him. After Omar's arrival they continued to build a guard chair near Ray's *caleta* each time they moved to a new camp, but the commandant gave orders that only one sentry should be there at a time. At least the evenings were quieter.

Eventually Ray and the guerrillas grew more comfortable with each other and their conversation became more relaxed. Omar, though capable of being a harsh leader, was kind to Ray and enjoyed his company. Sitting on a stump cleaning his rifle one hot, muggy September afternoon, he called Ray out of his shelter.

"Do you remember two French nationals who were kidnapped earlier this year?"

"Yes, in March, just a few weeks before you took me. I remember it was on a Sunday, because I got a call from the police in Puerto Lleras early in the morning, before church, saying the mayor needed to speak to me right away."

"What did the mayor say?" Omar probed.

"He wanted to know if anyone was missing from Lomalinda. It had been reported to him that two *gringos* had been taken by the guerrillas just on the other side of the river. I told him no, but that I would check to see if anyone was in the area from Bogotá."

"We found them, a man and a woman, walking on the other side of the river. They were staying in a hotel in Puerto Lleras. We thought they were your son and his girlfriend . . ."

Ray sat very still, feeling a knot of bitterness grow in his stomach. It surprised him that he could feel such intense anger, but he said nothing. He knew he could not confront the commandant, especially not in front of the others. To do so would be to risk reprisal.

"Of course we let them go," Omar added.

Ray looked at him but still said nothing.

As time wore on, the alternating routine of boredom and being on the move, tearing down and setting up camp, wore on everyone. Slowly Ray began to realize that the stress and anxiety of being held prisoner were making him very emotional. He overreacted to situations and cried easily. Every morning he woke up depressed and nervous, and he wondered how much longer he could survive before breaking down altogether. One Sunday morning, in prayer, it dawned on him that he needed to take the initiative to change his routine and add some positive experiences to his day. He was already studying his Bible several hours every morning but decided to add an exercise program to his regimen. He began jogging around the perimeter of the camp, guard close at hand, then followed his run with sit-ups and push-ups. And he asked Omar how he might be of use around camp.

"What can you do?" the commandant asked.

"I can repair things. Leo was complaining a couple weeks ago about a clock that isn't working," Ray answered.

"Leo, come here!" Omar yelled. Instantly, the guerrilla hurried up to Ray and Omar.

"Give Ramón your clock; he says he can fix it," Omar ordered.

To Ray's surprise, Leo pulled a wall clock—shaped like a keyhole and made of white plastic—out of his backpack. Ray opened it up, cleaned it, and fiddled with the many moving parts several times before finally getting it to run again.

Soon the guerrillas brought other broken articles to Ray. Repairing them was a challenge, since a short piece of wire, a flashlight bulb, his pen knife, a rag, and some occasional super glue and solder were his only tools. After a while the rag turned black from all the roach dirt and cobwebs he cleaned out of the various pieces of equipment. Once a cassette player fell off a mule, then the load the mule was carrying fell on top of it. Every plastic standoff support inside was broken, plus there were seventeen loose solder joints on the circuit board. Using a nail heated red-hot over a gasoline stove to solder the wires together, he was able to get the cassette player working again. Throughout his captivity Ray repaired a host of equipment, including tape players, radios, earphones, Walkmans and boom boxes, three television sets, and two solar panels. Sometimes the guerrillas stood around watching him, awed by his expertise. He used these opportunities to teach them about technical or scientific concepts, which opened the door to even more conversation.

Up to that point in his captivity, Ray had spent every waking moment thinking intensely about his freedom. Now, these opportunities to keep busy and do something constructive gave him much-needed relief and made him feel at peace. Still, a day didn't pass that he didn't daydream about freedom and his family: Was Rollin at school? Where was young Ray? How was Doris passing the time?

And he wondered about his own future. He frequently thought about a conversation he'd overheard between Arnoldo and some of the guerrillas, about an American who had worked with a nonprofit organization in the 1970s and had passed away in his home state about three years before. The commandant said he'd known the man, who had donned a dark green guerrilla uniform and traveled around with them in the La Macarena mountains for over a year. Contrary to public reports that he'd died of natural causes, the commandant said, he was killed because he'd talked about his experience.

Was that really true? Ray wondered. Maybe Arnoldo had just made it up to scare him. If true, what did it mean for him? Would they release him from captivity, only to kill him later? These and many other questions haunted Ray, sometimes to the point of mental exhaustion. Jorge's continued derision didn't help. He seemed to enjoy taunting the captive, especially about the possibility of the military breaking into camp and shooting him full of holes. Ray dreaded any contact with the guerrilla and stayed clear of him as much as possible.

Many times the guerrillas passed the evenings either listening to radios, watching a battery-operated television if one was available, or reading by candle or flashlight. Sometimes they read magazines or *La Voz,* a local publication, but more frequently they read pamphlets sent by the front about communism. They felt a kinship with the characters in Karl Marx's writings, fighting against capitalist exploitation. Like the followers of Marx, the guerrillas felt the injustice of the class system and dedicated themselves to changing the economic structure of the country. They saw themselves as the Robin Hoods of Colombian society— waging war against corruption and inequity—and it was only a matter of time before the guerrillas took over and set the country right.

Frequently they held political meetings by lamplight to boost morale. Ray had never heard such rhetoric as he heard at these meetings: hate the rich for keeping the rest of the country poor; hate the government for its debauchery; hate the military for killing their comrades; hate the auto-defenses for being the military's puppet. Aside from their own social ills, *norteamericanos* were their worst enemy—their capitalistic dollars were infiltrating the country, aiding its downfall as well as the guerrillas' extermination. The answer to the country's problems, they believed, was to overthrow the government, and to that end, the guerrillas were the people's army. The means to obtain these goals could be anything that would help the cause; the end result was paramount. The guerrillas had a fixed political agenda, Ray was told. Armed with AK-47s and other automatic rifles, pistols, and grenades, they were fearsome opponents for the national military and civilian auto-defense groups.

Sometimes they talked of gruesome battles they'd fought, of people killed or mutilated. During one such indoctrination session, on October 13, one of the guerrillas talked about shooting a policeman and seeing the top of his head flip up like the lid of a teakettle. Ray, who had been lying in his *caleta* and couldn't help but overhear their tirades, could stand the conversation no longer. Sitting up on his elbows, he leaned toward the table where the guerrillas were meeting. Seeing Ray looking at them, Leo said, "Yes Ramón, we're going to take power and put in a different system. A real rigid system."

"Leo," Ray said, exasperated, "that doesn't work anywhere in the world!"

"Oh, yes, it does!"

"Where?"

"In Cuba."

Ray laughed. "As I understand it, Cuba is a disaster economically!"

"Well," Maria piped up, "I'm going to kill someone anyway."

"Why?" Ray asked, astonished at her brazen remark.

"Because it makes me feel good."

"Well, it's a sin!"

As Ray's words hung in the air, the noise of a small, single-engine airplane broke the silence.

"Quick! Lights out!" Omar yelled.

Suddenly they could hear the plane directly overhead, very low, but they could see nothing. In a moment it was gone. The entire camp kept perfectly still for several minutes. Finally, Ray spoke up.

"That's really strange; there's no airstrip around here . . ."

"Really strange, huh?" Leo retorted. "That's either a surveillance plane or someone flying drugs. If it comes back we're going to shoot it down!"

They sat quietly for another fifteen minutes, but the plane did not return.

"Maybe they didn't see us," Leo said.

"Maybe," Omar replied.

The next morning nothing happened. Omar decided they must not have been spotted and were safe to remain where they were. But early the following morning two helicopters approached. They were troop carriers.

"Everyone, down!" Omar yelled. He crept over to Ray. "Get in your *caleta!* If they pass over, hopefully they won't see you."

Ray did what he was told and lay, heart pounding wildly, inside his shelter. Soon the choppers flew to one side of the woods camouflaging their camp and hovered momentarily in the air. Then the larger one, a Blackhawk, landed in the grassland while the smaller one circled around the field. Ray knew the Blackhawk was unloading troops and felt fear swelling up like a ball in his throat. *How do the guerrillas keep this up year after year?* he wondered. *How much longer can I keep this up?* Suddenly the irony of the situation struck him head-on: Here he was, hiding from the people who had sought to protect him and his companions year after year at Lomalinda. And protect them from whom? The very people he'd just spent the last several months with! In contemplation of this, he didn't know whether to laugh or cry.

In minutes the Blackhawk took off again, spraying machine gun fire as it passed nearby. *God, protect us!* Ray prayed, expecting to see wood chips flying through the trees at any moment. Everyone lay perfectly still for a very long time. Finally, Omar ordered a couple of guerrillas out of the camp to see where the military had landed and which direction they were heading. Shortly they reappeared—so quietly Ray had hardly noticed their leaving or returning—and reported back to the commandant, who decided they would lie low for the rest of the day and sneak out at night.

All that day Ray lay on his *caleta,* gripped by fear and anxiety. He had to escape! The military was only ten minutes away, if he could just get to them. . . . As the sun set among hues of pink and purple, he stuffed a handful of snacks into his shirt pocket—by now he was dressed in guerrilla garb so he could not be easily recognized through binoculars from overhead—and stole quietly down to the stream, toothbrush in hand. He squatted near the rushing water, dipping the brush in and brushing his teeth. As he did so he scanned up and down the stream for any movement that might indicate which way the military troops had settled. Suddenly he heard the snap of a shell loading into a gun, followed by the click of the safety release. He froze in place.

"I want to kill someone . . ." Maria mimicked her own words from two nights before.

Ray stood up slowly and turned to face the guerrilla, who held a loaded pistol by her side. Her legs were spread wide and slightly bent, ready for action.

"I'm brushing my teeth," Ray said, eying the gun.

Maria stared at him. "Get back to camp!" she hollered, pointing her gun in the direction of the campsite.

Heading back up the bank, Ray's mind was awhirl with confusion. In the center of the swirling mass of thoughts was fear so great he could hardly contain it—could he survive another week, another day, without getting killed or breaking down mentally? Images of Maria's gun aimed at the back of his head flashed through Ray's mind; he fought to resist the urge to turn around every couple of steps and see if the vision was correct. As the last remnants of sunlight pierced through the trees, one thought broke through all the rest, a thought not his own. *Peace I leave with you,*

Ray, my peace I give to you. Not as the world gives, give I to you. Let not your heart be troubled, neither be afraid (John 14:27). In the fullness of time, I will release you.

Ray knew God was speaking to him. He had not left him alone in the midst of this terrible hour.

Terrible News

August to December 1994

In August 1994, after a particularly disturbing meeting with the guerrillas, Ricardo arrived at Lomalinda looking very shaken. "The guerrillas are pressuring me; they want an immediate response or else!" Ricardo said. "I'm afraid they're going to kill him."

Then in late October Chaddy Stendal called SIL in Bogotá with distressing news: Ray had been the victim of an "accident." He would look into the details and get back to them. Meanwhile, the crisis committee waited anxiously for more news from the kidnappers. None came. December arrived before Chaddy called again. Yes, Ray had been killed, he said; unintentionally, according to his contacts. But two days later, another contact in the community called, notifying the committee that Ray would be freed that month or the following. Who were they to believe?

The crisis team convened to discuss the situation. Because of his contacts, Chaddy's testimony was compelling; yet their other source seemed equally sure of his information. The committee speculated whether there was any hope that the news from Chaddy was not true. After all, there was no hard evidence proving Ray was dead and no corroboration of the report from others. In fact, many plausible reasons existed to suggest that the supposition might be false: Chaddy's contacts could be genuinely mis-informed, or the story could be a cover-up on the guerril-las' part for their break in communication due to other causes.

In the end, the members of the crisis team decided to place their hope and faith in God, who alone was able to protect Ray in the midst of the most perilous circumstances. Still, as head of the crisis committee, George knew he needed to talk to Doris and tell her there was a chance Ray had been killed. She would want to know, and pray.

4

Beside the River

October to November 1994

By the rivers of Babylon,
There we sat down, yea, we wept
When we remembered Zion.
We hung our harps
Upon the willows in the midst of it.
For there those who carried us away
    captive required of us a song,
And those who plundered us required of us
    mirth,
Saying, "Sing us one of the songs of Zion!"

Psalm 137:1–3 NKJV

"*Ramón, get up!*" The guard shone a flashlight into the hostage's eyes, signaling the arrival of a new day.

"Luis," Ray said, shielding his eyes from the bright beam with his hand, "did you ever think that I might not like having that light in my eyes?"

The guerrilla ignored him. "Go wash up and then get packed. After breakfast we're leaving."

"Again? But we just—"

"I said go wash up!" Luis interrupted. "I don't need to explain anything to you!"

Ray groaned. Without looking at his watch he knew what time it was: 4:30, their usual wake-up hour. He'd better get moving so as not to arouse the guerrilla's bad temper, but he felt nervous and had a hard time engaging his mind to the task before him. *Lord, please help me to have a peaceful and pleasant day free of helicopters,* he prayed. Lying in his *caleta* a moment longer, he listened to the river, trying to release the tension already building in his neck and back. He thought of his wife and family and wept inwardly that he was facing the dawning of another day apart from them.

"Ramón!"

"I'm coming." Ray sighed. He emerged from his shelter and headed toward the stream to splash water on his face. What was he to do about Luis? A short guerrilla in his mid-twenties, Luis had been with Ray since the beginning of his captivity. When finally allowed to communicate with the hostage, he was friendly and helpful and enjoyed conversing about electronics and science. With a higher education than the rest of the guerrillas in camp, he was the only one who could explain some of the more difficult words Ray came across in his Spanish New Testament. But as time wore on, Luis grew bored and withdrawn. Frequently a hernia bothered him; at those times, he became extremely moody and argued with everyone. When guarding the captive, he treated Ray like a dog, barking orders at him about where to go and what to do. Even within the small space around his *caleta,* Ray had to ask Luis before speaking to the others standing or passing nearby. Always, the guerrilla gave these orders with his hand resting on his pistol and a threat in his voice. In God's time, Ray thought, Luis would be dealt with.

With breakfast behind them, Ray and the guerrillas broke camp and after another tedious walk set up housekeeping in a new location. In the previous weeks, Ray had gotten to know his captors' individual personalities and began learning how to deal with, or ignore, each one. But he had not fully acclimated to the variety of wildlife his new lifestyle afforded, especially the insects. Night and day, he had to be vigilant about watching for the huge conga ants with their poisonous venom; the hairy caterpillars, which, when rubbed against with the slightest touch, release a toxin equal to that of a cobra; fire ants whose sting sears the skin for hours; as well as the two-inch-long cockroaches that get into everything.

And he had to watch for rats. Their new campsite was in an especially dense tropical area, a perfect breeding ground for the rodents. The rusty tin cans, trash, and pieces of vinyl[1] strewn everywhere indicated some guerrillas had been there before—a rat's paradise.

By the time Ray's *caleta* was built on the perimeter of camp, evening had fallen once more. The nighttime brought on the usual noises, plus one he didn't immediately recognize. Lying on his freshly made mattress of palm leaves, he could hear something walking on the roof of his *caleta*.[2] Later that night he heard something on the ground near the foot of his shelter trying to climb up the leg of his bed. Swiftly Ray turned on his flashlight, shining it in the direction of the noise. There, two feet away, was an enormous rat about ten inches long excluding his tail! As the beam of his flashlight caught the animal's attention, Ray could see the black band circling each eye and shuddered.

"Guard!"

"What's the matter?" a girl named Merci replied. A simple, country girl, she was in love with the commandant and lived to beguile him.

Ray pointed toward the rat, which was apparently quite used to humans and continued its ascent up the leg of the hostage's *caleta*. Merci looked in the direction of the rodent and quaked. Then gathering her wits she ran for a shovel and slowly approached the animal. She raised the shovel over her head then dropped it down with all her might on top of the rodent's head, killing it. After that, Ray thought he heard more noises on several occasions and saw rats frequently in his dreams. A couple weeks later, Ray packed his things for another move. When he lifted up his rain poncho, which he had been sleeping on for extra padding, he found an abandoned rat's nest. He had been sleeping on top of a rat's nest!

After several nights in their new campsite, Ray awoke out of a sound sleep to a low rumbling growl followed by a snarl. Flashing his light into the darkness, he saw nothing. He turned his light off but lay acutely awake in his bed listening to every little sound, but he did not hear the noise again. The following morning he approached José.

"What kind of a sound does a panther make?" Ray asked, knowing the large cats are common to the jungle regions of South America. José responded with a roar that sounded similar to the sound Ray had heard the night before.

"Have you seen any around here?" Ray asked.

"No, but I've heard them. They're black and usually hunt at night, so they're very hard to see."

Ray went to bed that evening tired from lack of sleep the night before but alert to the noises around him. As the moon climbed high overhead, he heard a low growl, then another, followed by the familiar snarl. Bolting upright, he called out to José.

"Did you hear that?"

"Hear what?" José answered.

"That growl!"

With his rifle ready under one arm, José shone his flashlight into the surrounding trees but saw and heard nothing. "I think your mind is playing tricks on you," he said, turning off his light. The hostage lay back down, wondering if that were possible. No, he concluded, he knew what he'd heard. For the next couple weeks, Ray did not sleep well.

As Thanksgiving approached, they moved again, this time to a clean campsite near a wide river. With few mosquitoes and fresh fish to eat, it was the best location yet. A few days later, after scouting the surrounding area, José marched up to Ray. "Someone carved an *R* on that tree," he said, pointing to a tall tree near Ray's *caleta*. "Did you do that?" he demanded of the captive.

"No, *señor*," Ray responded. "Remember, there are others here whose names start with an *R*. I did that once before and you all got mad at me."

Unlike Arnoldo's response to the last time some initials were found on a tree, Omar appeared indifferent to the problem. "If it's meant for Ramón to be discovered, it won't be due to an *R* etched on a tree," he said.

Mauricio, an older guerrilla, nodded solemnly in agreement. He and a woman had been living a short distance outside the camp, receiving supplies and sending out orders, but he had joined Ray and the others after the near miss with the military a couple weeks before. He had been a guerrilla for eighteen years, and, listening to his stories, Ray gathered he was an experienced fighter. Yet he was fair to the captive and didn't bad-mouth him. Still, Ray perceived a ruthless side to him and remained leery.

"You're right," the hostage agreed. "It will be because God ordained it."

"If there is a God, he doesn't concern himself with the cares of this world," Mauricio scoffed. "Fate is what orders our lives."

"No," the captive persisted. "For instance, while traveling several years ago, I had set a bag on the floor of a taxi, and when I got out in the dark, I forgot it. The bag had some important things in it and I needed to find it, but after frantically searching for the taxi among forty others in the square, I finally gave up. That evening I put in a notice with *La Voz de los Llanos* radio station; there was nothing else I could do. Then I prayed and waited. Later that night, the taxi showed up with my bag!"

"That just means you were a good person at the time," Mauricio said.

"And now God is chastising you for doing something bad!" Luis chimed in.

"God is good; he doesn't work that way," Ray responded.

"If he's so good, then why are you out here in the woods with us?" Leo asked.

Ray had no ready answer to Leo's question and remained silent. He thought about Job in the Old Testament and realized that millennia later the same kind of human reasoning Job's friends used is still around. No, God does not work like that. Instead, Ray felt his predicament more akin to Joseph's, whose brothers had jealously sold him into slavery to get rid of him. Though the boy's prospects looked dismal at the time, God intended the situation for good and elevated Joseph to a command second only to the pharaoh so he could preserve his family from starvation. But how could he explain all this to the guerrillas, many of whom believed life and death lay in the hands of spirits?

Mauricio, especially, was a tough one to talk to about such things. As a young man he had traveled to Japan to study Eastern philosophy and entomology and the interaction between mankind and the world around him. Early in his career as a guerrilla, he was shot in the head by a military soldier and had a metal plate put in his skull. That he survived the ordeal only cemented his belief in fate, and now he held meetings with the other guerrillas, teaching them from his knowledge and experience.

Yet even in the midst of his calm, sophisticated demeanor, Mauricio's dark side would occasionally rise to the surface. A few days after Ray's exchange with the guerrillas about fate, Mauricio was sitting on his caleta listening to the radio when he heard a breaking news story about one hundred people who had recently died.

"Did you hear that? One hundred people, that's great!" the guerrilla beamed, thinking the deaths were due to a guerrilla attack. But listening to the broadcast further, he discovered the people had been victims of a plane crash rather than a conflict with guerrillas. To placate himself, he spent the rest of the afternoon on his *caleta* reading communist propaganda out loud. This disturbed Ray, whose own *caleta* was beside the guerrilla's, so he opened his Spanish New Testament with selected psalms and read aloud from the psalms. For several minutes the two grew louder and louder until Mauricio finally snapped his booklet shut.

"Wasn't that good, Ramón?"

"Yeah, that was really good, Mauricio. Now why don't you try reading something worthwhile?" Ray held his Bible out to the guerrilla.

Mauricio held out his hand to take the green leather book, then withdrew it and rolled over on his bed of sticks and leaves.

Finally, Thanksgiving Day arrived, but for the guerrillas and their hostage deep in the Colombian jungle, the day would be spent like any other. As Ray awoke with these thoughts in his mind, a wave of loss and depression washed over him. He longed for his usual family holiday traditions and couldn't bear facing the day with nothing to look forward to. Yet he knew his family would be praying for him and wanting him to join them at least in spirit. After his morning routine, Ray opened his Bible and read Romans 15. Coming to verse 13 he read aloud quietly, "May the God of hope fill you with all joy and peace as you trust in him, so that you may overflow with hope by the power of the Holy Spirit." *How to overflow with peace?* Ray wondered. Some mornings he woke up with a hymn or verse of Scripture filling his thoughts. This morning he would have to

91

create his own worshipful attitude. Dredging his memory for hymns, he decided to sing one of his favorites: "How Great Thou Art." Especially meaningful was the second verse.

> When through the woods and forest glades I wander
> and hear the birds sing sweetly in the trees,
> when I look down from lofty mountain grandeur
> and hear the brook and feel the gentle breeze.
>
> Then sings my soul, my Savior God, to thee;
> how great thou art, how great thou art!
> Then sings my soul, my Savior God, to thee:
> How great thou art, how great thou art!

The hours passed and the guerrillas went about their business, leaving Ray to himself. With few distractions, the captive spent his day meditating on some psalms, rereading a few beloved passages and randomly selecting others as his fingers scanned the pages. As he read, three specific passages stood out from the others, and Ray sensed God's still, small voice leaving its imprint on his heart. From Psalm 46, he sensed God telling him not to be afraid, for he was by the captive's side. From Psalm 121, he heard God promising him protection from harm. And from Psalm 146, he felt God speaking words of encouragement that someday he would be liberated from his jungle prison. Finally, he turned to Romans 4:21, an old favorite that suddenly came alive with new meaning. In a quiet whisper, he read aloud, "Being fully persuaded that God had power to do what he had promised."

Dead or Alive?

December 1994

The sun rose brilliant one early December morning and reflected off a layer of ice clinging to the grass and trees outside the sliding glass door that led to Doris's backyard. The last few days had been colder than normal for Waxhaw, and she was happy for the pile of wood stacked high beside the wood-burning stove. All morning she sat beside the fire, alternating between reading and praying and watching the cardinals and blue jays outside the glass. As she stoked the fire with a poker, turning the wood over to burn more evenly, the phone rang.

"Hello?"

"Hi, Doris; it's George. How are you this morning?"

"Oh, fine, just sitting here by the fire."

"Well, I have some news I feel I must tell you, but I want to preface it by saying I don't know if it's true or not . . ."

Doris, who had stood up to answer the phone, drew out a kitchen chair and sat down.

"It's about Ray. We've heard some disturbing reports that he may have been killed, but we haven't been able to confirm anything."

Tears filled Doris's eyes. She took off her glasses and brushed the tears away with a sweep of her forefinger.

"Doris?" George asked, engulfed in the awkward silence of the moment. Like Ray, Doris was quiet and reflective, and it was hard to tell what she was thinking.

"I'm listening," Doris replied.

"Okay, well, you know we've been in contact with a variety of people, and one of our sources told us that Ray had been in an accident back in October. We don't know what kind, or if it's even true. We're trying to find out more, but you know, it's slow going."

Doris sighed deeply. Not one to be overwrought by emotion, she tried to take the news in stride. "I know you're doing everything you can, George. I'll be all right. You'll let me know as soon as you hear anything?"

"The moment I hear anything, I'll let you know."

Doris hung up the phone and slipped back to the fire. Later that afternoon she would have to go in to work at the JAARS center, she thought, and slumped into the chair.

Christmas Greetings

December 1994

In the midst of rumors of Ray's death and silence from his captors, the crisis team came up with two ideas they hoped would entice the guerrillas to confirm whether or not Ray was alive and reopen negotiations. One was to produce a flyer to be distributed by hand in Puerto Lleras and the surrounding area, reminding people of Ray's continuing hostage situation. Suggesting that the best Christmas present for the people of Puerto Lleras would be for Ray Rising to walk free, the flyer went into production immediately.

Second, the crisis committee decided to arrange for Doris to be interviewed on a radio station that aired in the area where Ray was believed to be held. After debating the pros and cons of such a move and deciding it was worth the effort if Ray or his captors or both heard the broadcast, they put out feelers to the radio community and news stations around Villavicencio and the surrounding plains to the east. Eventually a taped interview was arranged with the radio news show *Radio Periódico al Minuto (Up to the Minute Radio Magazine),* airing over *La Voz de los Llanos* (The Voice of the Plains) in Villavicencio.

As the interview approached, George Kavanaugh went to Waxhaw and met Doris with the list of questions to be asked; together they reviewed her answers. After a postponement due to a late-breaking news story in Villavicen-cio, the interview finally took place on December 16.

As a technician set up the speakerphone and ran some tests to make sure the equipment was working properly, Doris fidgeted nervously in her seat inside the conference room at the JAARS center in Waxhaw. After saying a prayer and gaining her composure, she was ready for the interview. Moments later she heard the Spanish-speaking voice of a Colombian broadcaster coming through the phone:

Announcer: *Radio Periódico al Minuto,* the Voice of the Llanos, has radio contact at this moment with the wife of Mr. Ramón Rising, who has been held for some time. He is a functionary of the Summer Institute of Linguistics and was working in the zone of Puerto Lleras here in the Department of Meta in Lomalinda when he was captured. We will greet Mrs. Doris Rising who is in the U.S. Doris, a very good morning.

Doris: Good morning, sir.

Announcer: Ladies and gentlemen, I will tell you that we will utilize a translator. Doris, although she understands Spanish, does not speak it very well. Mrs. Mary Smith will loan us her service to do the translating. We will greet, then, Mary, good morning.

Mary: Good morning, sir.

Announcer: Very well, Mary. Please ask Doris how much time they have been in Colombia, together with Ramón?

Doris: We have been in Colombia off and on for about twenty years. We worked for over eleven years at Lomalinda and then went to work in another country, and then almost six years ago we returned to Colombia again.

Announcer: What was Ramón's work, or what is Ramón's work in Lomalinda?

96

Doris: He was very active in communicating with the people in Puerto Lleras. He donated funds to make sure that the poor children in Puerto Lleras would have books and uniforms for school, and if there were some poor families that needed medical help or food, he would try to help them also.

Announcer: Doris, has Ramón always worked at Lomalinda, or has he worked in other parts of Colombia?

Doris: No, we have always lived at Lomalinda.

Announcer: How many children do you have, and have they also been in Colombia?

Doris: We have two sons and our youngest just came home yesterday from school in Chicago, and it will be great having him here for the holidays. Our oldest son is working and he travels quite a bit, but when he is home he has been a great comfort to me.

Announcer: How long has Ramón been captive?

Doris: Since March 31 of this year.

Announcer: If Ramón is listening, Doris, what message would you have for him, and also for his captors?

Doris: I love you a lot and I miss you very much and look forward to your coming home, and I hope it's soon. It has been a difficult time, but God has given us strength.

Announcer: Do you want to say something to Ramón's captors?

Doris: I don't know why this has happened, but I am sure no harm was intended to my husband. I have appreciated the fact that you have respected Ray's life, that you have cared for him, and that you have allowed him to send letters to me. I am confident that if you communicate again, this can be resolved. The

97

only thing that interests me and the Instituto is that you release Ramón.

Announcer: Doris, would you like to tell a little more of how things have been going for you since Ramón has been taken?

Doris: Okay. We returned to the United States and we have been able to be with our families. I have had to take the responsibility of getting our youngest son started in the university. I have also tried to be an encouragement to Ray's eighty-nine-year-old mother. She is blind and in frail health. She doesn't understand why her son is in this situation, and it is very hard to give her information. I don't have much information to give, and yet I try to encourage her.

Announcer: The grief that is reflected in the voice of Mrs. Doris Rising, wife of Ramón Rising, who has been captured since March 1994 in a section near the Municipality of Puerto Lleras. This then is the testimony by way of a telephone conversation from the U.S., in which she asks that the life of her husband be respected, and that he be returned as soon as possible.

This has been an exclusive interview with the wife of one of the North Americans captured here in the Department of Meta. The telephone communication was made between Villavicencio and the U.S.[3]

The interview concluded, Doris carefully placed her purse strap over her shoulder and went home, hoping Ray and his captors would hear one of the broadcasts to be aired the week before Christmas.

Lomalinda, where Ray and Doris lived and worked for SIL.

Lomalinda Lake and the surrounding jungle.

Ray at his workbench in the radio department at Lomalinda.

Ray and Doris in front of their home.

A view of Puerto Lleras from across the Ariari River.

Ray visiting a nursery in Puerto Lleras.

Ray giving two children from Puerto Lleras a ride on his motorcycle.

The back gate where Ray was abducted.

The guerrillas used dugout canoes such as these to transport Ray during his captivity.

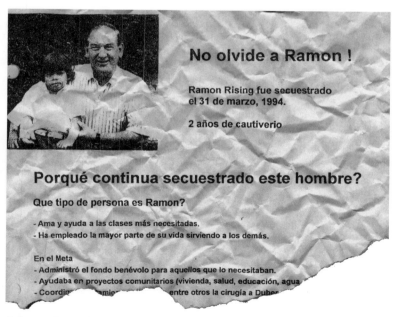

No olvide a Ramon !

Ramon Rising fue secuestrado el 31 de marzo, 1994.

2 años de cautiverio

Porqué continua secuestrado este hombre?

Que tipo de persona es Ramon?

- Ama y ayuda a las clases más necesitadas.
- Ha empleado la mayor parte de su vida sirviendo a los demás.

En el Meta
- Administró el fondo benévolo para aquellos que lo necesitaban.
- Ayudaba en proyectos comunitarios (vivienda, salud, educación, agua
- Coordin   mie   entre otros la cirugía a Dube

A flyer airdropped by the crisis committee on March 30, 1996.

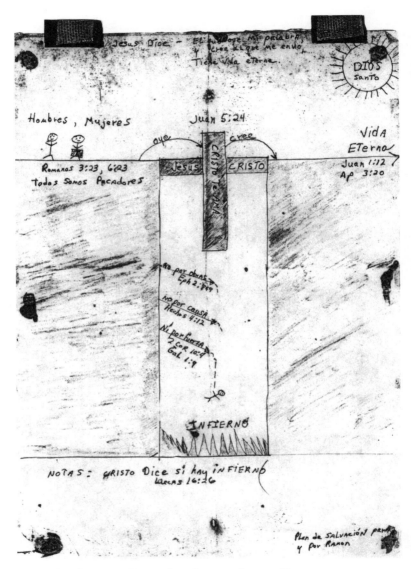

The bridge illustration Ray used to witness to the guerrillas.

Ray and Doris are reunited in the Charlotte airport.

Ray Jr. greeting Ray in San Martín after Ray's release.

Ray and his family a few weeks after his return. From left to right: Rollin, Ray Jr., Ray, Doris.

5

The Holidays

December 1994 to January 1995

> For the eyes of the LORD run to and fro throughout the whole earth, to show Himself strong on behalf of those whose heart is loyal to Him.
>
> 2 Chronicles 16:9 NKJV

December came, and except for a handful of sporadic rainstorms that passed quickly, the weather remained dry as well as hot. The motionless air allowed Ray to hear noises usually masked by the otherwise frequent breeze: the cutter ants devouring everything in their path, the marching ants parading along a trail through the thick underbrush, even the muted sounds of exotic birds flitting from one tree branch to the next.

With the approaching holidays, military action in the area had died down, and Omar felt relatively secure in their secluded jungle haven. That meant no tearing down camp, no packing up, no building furniture. As much as Ray hated these activities and the uncertainty they brought, the boredom of hour after hour with nothing to do was worse. Ray kept busy each morning with his routine of prayer, Bible meditation, and exercise, but the rest of the day crawled by. The guerrillas kept mostly to themselves, taking turns performing perfunctory duties around the camp and cleaning their weapons, over and over again. Here and there, conversation, a joke, or laughter would erupt, breaking the dull cadence of the day, but for the most part Ray was alone with his thoughts—sometimes the worst enemy of all.

As he lay on his back on his *caleta,* his mind wandered. *What would I be doing today if I were home in Lomalinda? Today's Friday . . . or is it Saturday? Maybe Doris and I would do some Christmas shopping. I hate Christmas shopping! Then Doris would sit at the table preparing her greeting cards and would ask me to help her sign them. Why didn't I do that more often? Okay, gotta get away from Lomalinda . . . What if I were back in Waxhaw . . . chopping wood for the wood stove maybe, or watching the cardinals in the back yard. Maybe there'd be snow flurries . . .* Just then a trickle of sweat ran down from his hairline and dripped into his ear. Ray shook his head and wiped the moisture out of his ear with his sleeve.

God, what am I doing here? My family needs me. . . . I need them! Ray rolled over, letting his head fall into his crossed arms, and sobbed quietly. He didn't want the guerrillas to see him crying; to them it was a sign of weakness. For the next hour he cried out to God, in anger and resentment combined with tears of sorrow.

With each passing day Christmas drew ever nearer and Ray withdrew more and more into his thoughts. Each sunrise, this same pattern repeated itself—breakfast, Bible reading, prayer, exercise, then internal dialogue that carved a rut in his thinking of resentment, loneliness, and despair. *Where will it all end? Is there any hope to be found here? Must I spend Christmas away from the ones who love me?* Sometimes God brought relief to his internal anguish in the form of a bird chirping a bold greeting or a friendly word from his captors. Sometimes he did not, nudging Ray to learn to trust in God alone for peace and not his external circumstances.

On December 13, Ray was resting on his *caleta,* guarded by one of the female guerrillas. His Bible lay open on his lap to Luke 10, the parable of the Good Samaritan. As he read the passage, the meaning of the story came alive as never before. Looking around the camp at his guerrilla captors, he realized God called him to show mercy to them, just as the Samaritan man had done to his Jewish "neighbor." *But not grudgingly,* Ray thought. *Let all that you do be done in love (1 Cor. 16:14 NKJV).*

Just then a muffled gunshot rang out not far away. Ray thought nothing of it and continued reading, as the guerrillas frequently practiced target shooting or hunted game for the evening meal. But a few minutes later Mauricio came hobbling up a hill toward camp with no weapon and one unbooted foot dangling in midair. His foot dripping with blood, Mauricio groaned as he fell into his shelter beside Ray's. The guard ran over to the injured man, yelled for one of the others to bring Leo, then returned to her post.

"What happened to Mauricio? Did he cut himself?" Ray asked with a concerned frown.

The guard shook her head and pointed to her M1 carbine.

"He shot himself?"

"But don't tell anybody I told you so!"

After a few minutes Leo arrived. Quickly, he began digging into the wound, cleaning out the bone fragments.

"Owww!" Mauricio yelled, kicking his leg into the air. "Don't you have anything to numb it?"

"No, but you need to hold still," Leo growled, trying to concentrate on his work. The other guerrillas took hold of Mauricio's leg and forced it flat. Mauricio strained against them, becoming angrier by the second.

"Let me go over and talk to him," Ray implored his guard. She looked over at the wounded guerrilla, then motioned to Ray to get up. Ray pressed in between two guerrillas and looked at Mauricio's foot. There, right above the big toe, was a bullet hole the size of a quarter. Kneeling beside the guerrilla, Ray took one of his hands and squeezed it. "Lord Jesus, I pray right now for Mauricio, my neighbor, asking that you will help him and give him peace. Please make him more comfortable while Leo works on his foot."

"Save your prayers!" Leo snapped. Ray ignored him. For several minutes he held the guerrilla's hand and prayed silently. Finally, Leo pulled the last stitch through Mauricio's skin and tugged lightly, then knotted the thread. The guerrillas took their hands off their comrade and went back to their business, but Ray stayed by his side.

"I think your prayer helped," Mauricio said in a raspy voice. "I felt a little more at ease."

Leo only clicked his tongue in disgust. After concluding his work, the guerrilla approached Ray as he again lay in his *caleta*. "You're wasting your time on all that Christian mumbo jumbo."

"God is real, and prayer is communication with the Creator of the universe. I don't see it as a waste of time."

"What's real is what's happening here and now. Nothing else matters," Leo retorted.

"What if you're wrong? What are you going to say at the judgment?"

"That I brought salvation to the masses."

"Is that what you believe?" Ray looked shocked.

"In the apostles' time, people knew how to work magic," Leo said. "God had nothing to do with it."

This discussion dragged on for two hours, with Ray trying to convince the guerrilla of the validity of the power of God and the Holy Spirit. Finally, he realized his words fell on deaf ears. "Friend, there's no solution for you," he said, and lay back down on his bed.

The next day Nate, who had overheard the debate and Ray's ending comment, asked the captive if he had lost his temper. "No, but if a person blasphemes the Holy Spirit, there is no hope for him."

"What do you mean, blaspheming the Holy Spirit?" Nate inquired.

"If someone calls the Holy Spirit a liar and attributes God's work to the devil, he is blaspheming or desecrating God's name. His soul is in danger, and I feel he needs to be told so," Ray answered.

Finally, Christmas Eve arrived. Knowing the day could not possibly bring any of the normal warmth or happiness of the holiday season, Ray dreaded the impending hours. But he knew that his family would want him to make the best of it and that God expected him to be content in whatever situation in which he found himself. For the next few hours he whiled away the time singing hymns and Christmas carols softly under his breath and reading every passage he could remember from the Bible that spoke of the Savior's birth. If he listened intently, he could hear the music being played on the guerrillas' radios and tape decks. Though not the traditional Yuletide music, it lifted his spirits.

Lying inside the mosquito netting of his *caleta* in the sweltering late-afternoon sun, Ray could hear a broadcast emitting from the radio in the *caleta* next to his—*Radio Periódico al Minuto* airing over *La Voz de los Llanos* from Villavicencio. He'd heard the program many times before while sitting on his porch in Lomalinda. It was one of the best sources around for local news and updates of happenings in the surrounding area. As the introduction to the show continued, the guerrilla inside the *caleta* got up and left, leaving the radio on with the volume turned up. This surprised Ray, as both Arnoldo and Omar strictly enforced the rule that no radio or television newscast should be left on unattended (they thought their hostage might hear some disturbing news about himself and create problems for them), and to do so invited disciplinary action. *Well, it's Christmas Eve,* the captive thought.

The program began. Ray recognized the voice of the announcer, followed by a soft female voice, then another, also female. An interview? As he listened intently, a wave of shock coursed through Ray's body—one of the women was speaking English! *Who is that talking . . . Doris? Have I been listening to Spanish so long I don't recognize her voice?* Ray wondered. He ran over to the radio to hear it more clearly. Risky business, but he didn't care. This was too important to be concerned with the guerrillas' reaction.

"If Ramón is listening, Doris, what message would you have for him, and also for his captors?" the announcer asked in Spanish, which the other female voice interpreted into English.

"I love you a lot and I miss you very much," Doris's voice responded, "and look forward to your coming home, and I hope it's soon. It has been a difficult time, but God has given us strength."

"Do you want to say something to Ramón's captors?" the announcer repeated.

"I don't know why this has happened," Doris went on, "but I am sure no harm was intended to my husband. I have appreciated the fact that you have respected Ray's life, that you have cared for him, and that you have allowed him to send letters to me. I am confident that if you communicate again, this can be resolved. The only thing that interests me and the *Instituto* is that you release Ramón."

The broadcast ended. Ray's eyes sparkled, and he grinned in delight; it was all he could do to keep from shouting, but fear of what the guerrillas might think kept him quiet. Suddenly he noticed Leo, who had been guarding him and had seen everything. For the first time he thought about the repercussions of his actions, but instead of reprimanding him, the guerrilla said, "Keep on listening; maybe they'll repeat it. Our goal is that you can go home."

Ray listened for a while longer, then went back to his *caleta* and lay down, stunned by the message he had just heard. Finally, he released the sobs he'd felt building inside, of shock and overwhelming joy mingled together. How great a God he served, that he would allow Ray to hear his wife's voice on Christmas Eve! His prayers had not bounced off the walls of heaven, as he had so often felt. God had heard them, every one, and had expressed his love and compassion in a way that let Ray know God had not forgotten him.

The rest of Christmas Eve and all of Christmas Day, Ray's spirits soared. For months Jorge had railed at him about his wife forgetting he existed and finding another man, and though Ray didn't believe him, he was elated to hear Doris express her love for him. For hours he lay on his *caleta,* daydreaming about his family around the dinner table and the sights and smells of turkey with all the trimmings while waiting for his own Christmas meal. Maria and José had been gone for several hours the day before, and now a large chicken sizzled inside the makeshift oven. Ray wondered if the farmer or butcher had received payment for the bird, but kept his question to himself.

After hours of fussing and fuming under the kitchen tarp, Maria finally called everyone to dinner. As he headed toward the stream to wash his hands, the smell of roasted chicken induced sharp hunger pangs in Ray's stomach. Famished, he eyed the picnic table made of rough-hewn planks. Turkey or no turkey, it looked like a regular feast compared to the usual fare of beans, tortillas, and rice. A ring of vegetables—carrots and potatoes and yuca—surrounded the roasted chicken. To the side, in a large metal bowl, polished red apples shone in the afternoon sun. Best of all, several brightly decorated tins filled to the brim with Christmas cookies lay nestled among the other victuals.

"Hey, good job!" Nate, a good-looking youth cheered, raising a bottle of wine in one hand and brandy in the other. The guerrillas filled their cups all around. Though they never became intoxicated in front of Ray, they did get drunk on occasion when they visited the homes of the *campesinos*. Ray always knew when they were returning from one of those visits, usually late at night, as a loud ruckus invariably announced their arrival.

After the meal and throughout the rest of the afternoon, Ray and his captors played chess and other games, laughing and listening to their Walkmans and boom boxes. But as evening approached, the festive atmosphere in the camp grew melancholy, and the music reflected the change in mood. *Perhaps they're reminiscing about their own Christmases past,* Ray mused. Popular music in Colombia, which originates from Panama, Mexico, and Venezuela as well as Colombia, is always rich and passionate, whether it is a boisterous dance song or a haunting love *balada* such as *"Rey de Despecho"* ("King of Rejection"). Previously, Ray never understood how Colombians could be so swayed by the music they listened to, but watching the guerrillas croon along with the tunes pouring from the radio, he realized that for these people it's a way of escape from a very difficult life.

As darkness encircled the camp, the music died down; except for the croaking of hundreds of frogs, silence enveloped the jungle. Unable to sleep with thoughts of his family tumbling around in his head, Ray rolled from side to side trying to settle into his *caleta*. But it was no use; his mind kept spinning and refused to allow him to sleep. Slowly, softly, like a parrot feather suspended on a breeze, a melody began drifting through the camp. Listening carefully, Ray recognized José's voice. An incurable romantic, José loved music and frequently composed his own ballads in his free time. *This must be one of his new songs,* Ray thought. He focused on the soothing lilt of the guerrilla's voice and allowed the strain to calm him. The song, about a mother's love for her son, reminded Ray of his own eighty-nine-year-old mother living in Minnesota. Thoughts of her singing hymns at his bedside when he was a small boy flooded his mind, and he fell asleep with a prayer on his lips that he would see his mother again.

The week between Christmas and New Year's crawled by without incident. With the dry season now in full swing, the ground dried up from its perpetually muddy condition and the mosquito population died down. Military activity seemed at a lull, so Omar felt relatively safe remaining at their present campsite. Aside from daily camp maintenance, there was very little for the guerrillas to do except clean and reclean their automatic weapons, and absolutely nothing for Ray to occupy himself with. Then, just as the boredom became almost unbearable, Maria and José disappeared again just as they had right before Christmas. As insignificant as that seemed, Ray knew something was about to happen and the tension was just enough to break the monotonous cycle. "Where did Maria and José go?" he inquired. But his question was met with only giggles from his captors.

Finally, the two returned with a large bale of straw and a spare camouflage-green guerrilla uniform. On New Year's Eve the mood in the camp picked up again, as Ray's captors began stuffing the uniform with the fragrant yellow straw. An hour passed and then another, and finally the stuffed figure began to take shape. The guerrillas fashioned a head and affixed it to the plump body, even managing to attach a pair of boots to the pant legs. Black plastic tarp material was transformed into hair and a mustache. All the while, the guerrillas laughed as though they had swallowed a secret and it was trying to escape. As a finishing touch, they nestled a whittled pump shotgun into the "sling" created by tying the dummy's hands together. They stepped back to admire their workmanship. Noticing the similarity between the whittled replica and the shotgun Leo carried, Ray wondered how Leo's Winchester-made gun—a carryover from the Vietnam era—had made it to the present-day backwoods of Colombia. He had no complaints, however; the gun had come in handy for shooting the wild game he sometimes enjoyed.

"It almost looks real," Maria said.

"Watch out! He's going to shoot you!" Jorge taunted.

Maria smirked. "It's got your name on the barrel," she said, and walked away. Jorge's eyes followed her down the trail, then he walked up to the dummy and inspected the rifle.

As supper concluded that night, Omar asked for some popcorn, and Leo jumped up to prepare it. As he passed the table, Omar gazed at Leo and then at the stuffed mannequin now hanging from a nearby chonta palm, its boots dangling in the tree's thorny roots.

"Ramón, who does that look like?" Omar gestured at the mannequin with his chin. Ray looked at the dummy with its bulging midsection and slick hair and mustache.

"It looks like Leo!" Ray responded with a laugh. The entire camp burst out in a fit of laughter, except of course for Leo, who sat sulking beside the stove shaking a pot of popping corn.

As at Christmas, after supper Ray played some games with the guerrillas while festive music blared through the trees. But unlike the week before, the activities stopped early and Ray was told to go to bed while several of the guerrillas left the camp for a party at a local *campesino's* house. *Will they return by the ten o'clock curfew?* Ray wondered, fighting to stay awake and see. Instead, he dropped quickly off to sleep. Later that night, he was jerked awake by a loud commotion at the other end of camp. With the near-full moon illuminating the giant jungle trees, Ray saw a handful of figures filing into the camp. Sliding his flashlight under his wool blanket, he turned on the light and checked the time. *Eleven-thirty—Omar will have them digging holes in the morning!* he thought.

It had grown still again and for quite a while Ray lay awake wondering what the new year would bring. He was just about to drift off to sleep again when a loud crash caused his eyes to fly wide open. *Crash . . . crash . . . crash!* The noise grew louder and louder and was joined by the sound of metal striking metal. *What in the world?* Ray thought, breaking into a cold sweat. He sat up in his *caleta* and gazed through the mosquito netting at the line of torches approaching him. *Is this the beginning of some cruel funeral march?* he wondered. Suddenly all eight guerrillas encircled him, some holding flaming torches while the others banged pot lids like cymbals or tapped serving spoons on metal bowls. Bringing up the rear, José's short, lithe body kept time with a harmonica pressed to his lips.

"What's going on?" Ray gasped. Then he remembered the traditional New Year's Eve ritual. He'd forgotten all about it! Slipping on his boots, he got up from his *caleta* and watched as the guerrillas serenaded him. Finally, Nate called out, "Speech!"

Ray felt obliged to respond but struggled for the right words. After a pause, he lifted his fist and began, "To the new year!" The guerrillas responded by banging on their improvised instruments.

"Let's burn the old year and leave it behind us and welcome a new year of peace for Colombia!" That was a safe salute, Ray thought, as peace was the heart's desire of every Colombian. The guerrillas cheered and banged their pans again in unison, then Omar stepped forward. He poured oil on the disarmed dummy, then lit it on fire with his torch. As the mannequin blazed, the guerrillas danced wildly around the camp with their torches, clanging pots and pan lids. As with most traditions, the burning of the old year in

Colombia was so repetitious that most people didn't think twice about what it symbolized. Up until that night Ray had never seen the ritual carried out with such gusto and had given very little thought to it. Now, as smoke swirled in black ringlets against the moonlit sky, he raised a sincere prayer to God: *Please bring peace to Colombia!*

Hope

For weeks after the radio broadcast, Doris hoped the guerrillas would release her husband or at least yield information about his well-being. As time went on, however, her hope turned into despair worsened by a hard-hitting cold. She spent many long hours of wakefulness at night praying for her husband. If she couldn't sleep, at least she could use the time constructively.

Rollin, attending Moody Bible Institute in Chicago, struggled through this time too. Run down from worry, he wanted to quit school and come home. Doris encouraged him to see it through, saying she would pray for him and ask others to do the same. A few days later he called saying he was feeling better and would stick it out.

On January 24, 1995, Doris received a letter by fax from George Kavanaugh. Seeing his name on the header, her heart filled with dread. Would it contain news of Ray's demise? In her prayers over the past few weeks, she'd sensed an unexplainable feeling that he was alive but had no foundation for thinking so. Hurriedly, she read the letter.

> . . . A contact with the Colombian Red Cross, who has been checking out rumors regarding Ray, received word indirectly that he is okay, though the details are

119

skimpy. Another report seems to indicate that he has been moved out of the immediate area but is alive. This is very comforting information, as another contact insists that he died a couple months ago. Then, within several days after that news, yet another contact came forward to say very specifically that he is alive! We still have no confirmation of any of these reports but are ever prayerful that he is indeed alive and well. . . .

Doris stuffed the letter into the folder where she kept all correspondence from the crisis committee. It was upsetting that so many weeks of intense effort to learn of Ray's condition had yielded such contradictory results. Still, a feeling lingered in the back of her mind that Ray was alive, and she knew she had to cling to that hope. She poured herself a cup of tea, then settled into a chair to look through the rest of the mail. Each day brought a letter or card from a friend, even strangers, filled with well wishes and prayerful thoughts for Ray and the family. What an encouragement! As she sifted through the stack, a postcard caught her eye. On the front was a quote from Pamela Reeve: "Faith is: Recognizing that God is the Lord of time when my idea of timing doesn't agree with His." *That will go on the refrigerator,* she thought, and set it aside.

After looking through the mail, Doris opened up a book given to her by a friend, *Unto the Hills* by Billy Graham. She turned to the dog-eared page and read:

It is reassuring to know that God is still all powerful, that nothing touches my life without His permission. Things happen to me that I cannot understand, but I never doubt God's love. In the hour of trial I may not be able to see His design, but I am confident it must be in line with His purpose.[1]

6

To Church

January to February 1995

> How then shall they call on Him in whom they have not believed? And how shall they believe in Him of whom they have not heard? And how shall they hear without a preacher? And how shall they preach unless they are sent? As it is written: "How beautiful are the feet of those who preach the gospel of peace, who bring glad tidings of good things!"
>
> Romans 10:14–15 NKJV

December, the month that marks the beginning of the dry season, had brought a dramatic drop in rainfall. Now, with the new year behind them and the stream they had been camping beside for several weeks drying up, it became necessary to move to a larger river. For a few days, a pair of the guerrillas scouted the area until a suitable site was found; the next week everyone packed up and headed across the *llanos* to another river several hours away. It was nice to travel through the grass without having it mash down with every soggy footstep. The tall blades seemed to stretch toward the sun as the camouflaged party pressed along. Ray felt like an adventurer blazing a new path through virgin territory. *This must have been what it was like for the families moving west across the American prairie,* he thought.

After leaving the *llanos* and walking through thick wooded undergrowth for an hour, they ran into a large river that babbled cheerfully as the water cascaded over stones near the water's edge. A small beach lay beside the river with a fish-laden spring nearby. Fresh fish! A perfect spot to camp. On January 10, 1995, the second in command of the front arrived. A young man of about thirty, slender build with dark hair and eyes, he gathered the guerrillas together and reviewed some of their propaganda material, encouraging them not to lose heart in the cause or in their current assignment. Then he approached the captive.

"How are they treating you? How's the food?" he asked Ray.

"Pretty good; I don't have any complaints."

"You're going to have to wait a little while longer."

"Okay," Ray said, "but it would be nice to receive some correspondence from my wife." The commander walked away, leaving Ray to ponder the meaning of his comment about waiting. Was something else going on in the country that was affecting his captivity that neither he nor SIL knew about?

The next day the commander came up to Ray again, just before leaving the camp.

"Is there anything you need?"

"A radio would be nice, and a newspaper occasionally to pass the time," Ray responded, hoping to hear some news about national events.

"You're keeping a diary, aren't you?"

"No, they won't let me write anything."

The commander raised his eyebrows, then nodded his head good-bye. A week later Omar brought Ray a notebook and pen. From that point on he kept track of the number of days in captivity and wrote daily notes about the weather and his devotions, his exercise regimen, and anecdotes about the guerrillas, using code words to identify each one.

Not long after the commander's visit, on January 24, Omar was replaced by another commandant, his cousin, Jaime. As Omar gathered up his things, Ray approached him.

"I wanted to thank you before you left," Ray said. "Things have been much easier since you came. Please excuse me for any mistakes."

"Don't even think about it," Omar responded emphatically. "I may see you again; then again I may not. They may release you! Take care, Ramón." With that the slender guerrilla tossed a pack over his shoulder and headed out of camp, taking Luis with him! Watching the pair leave camp, Ray's heart leapt for joy—though he was sorry to see his friend go, he was delighted not to have to deal with Luis's attempts at controlling him any longer.

At about five-foot-eight—the same height as Omar— Jaime looked much more formidable due to his husky build. A short beard and mustache framed his rigid lips. After a customary inspection of the unit, he approached Ray, sizing him up.

"Hello, I am Jaime," he said with some hesitation.

Ray nodded.

"So, how have they been treating you so far?"

"Everything has been adequate," Ray answered. "They have taken good care of me and protected me from danger. Look, I want you to know that I don't harbor any hatred toward anyone, and I'm not your enemy."

"I know that." For a long moment Jaime stared at the captive. Ray felt uneasy and fidgeted in his *caleta*.

"Do you recognize me?" Jaime finally said.

Ray looked hard at the new commandant. "No, I don't. Should I?"

"I've been in your house."

"Did you come with anyone else?"

"Yeah . . ." Jaime hesitated, then said abruptly, "Well, if you need anything, let me know." With that the commandant turned on his heels and walked away. For several days Ray searched his memory, trying to remember when he might have seen this man before. Slowly a faded recollection came to him of a time when a couple of Colombian men had come for a tour. Ray, who had been their guide, had offered them a cold drink and cookies in his home afterward. Clean shaven at the time, Jaime was one of those men. *He was in my house eating my food!* Ray thought. *God, what reward is there in doing good if this is the result?* Then he remembered Uncle Cam, founder of SIL, who, teaching that Christians are to serve everybody, always had exciting stories to tell of how God used his kindness to make friends and open new doors for Bible translation. *Not my kind of excitement,* Ray thought, *but there sure is a lot of room for service!*

February arrived and the seasonal breeze that normally caused the *llanos* to sway lazily turned into a steady hot wind that pressed the grass flat and died down only at sunset. The evenings, however, were comfortable and invigorating. Without the canopy of clouds that is so common during the rainy season, stars twinkled here and there where the treetops gave way to the night sky. The jungle came alive in the dry season with chirps and croaks and buzzes and an occasional growl, as creatures of all shapes and sizes took advantage of the more clement weather. Though bedtime remained the same, Ray found it difficult to sleep. The frogs were especially noisy.

The daytime, too, was full of noise, as the winds picked up and caused giant chonta palm fronds to break off and drop one hundred feet to the ground, crashing against other trees along the way. Hoping the tarp and mosquito netting that surrounded his *caleta* would act as a windbreak, Ray spent a good part of his days in bed thinking about his captors. By this time he knew why he had been kidnapped. The guerrillas had taken him, perhaps in retaliation against the presence of U.S. soldiers in the country, but certainly in hopes of gaining a ransom that would help fund their activities. They believed they were in complete control of the situation. But God in his sovereign wisdom and love had allowed him to be taken for one reason alone: to bring the gospel of Christ to the guerrillas. Misguided and longing for a sense of belonging, these young men and women needed God, and God loved them.

Ray knew he was not alone in his predicament; at that very moment, in other parts of Colombia, guerrilla forces held five men hostage from New Tribes Mission, a missionary organization based out of Florida.[1] Ray didn't know any of these men personally but felt a common bond with them, knowing that God had called them all to the same task of sharing Christ with these otherwise unreachable people. But at what cost? Chet Bitterman, a translator with SIL, had been kidnapped by guerrillas in January 1981. Politically motivated, that hostage situation ended with his death only weeks after his abduction.[2] Would the New Tribes men die as Chet had? Would he die?

The LORD *gives freedom to the prisoners (Ps. 146:7 NKJV),* Ray reminded himself, trying to shake free of these tortuous thoughts. Over the past few months he had learned he had to control his thoughts if he was going to survive, otherwise he would be swallowed up by despair so deep he might be emotionally scarred forever. *In the meantime, I need to be doing God's will,* he told himself.

In late February, the dry, seasonal breeze stopped and the stagnant air hung heavy in the noonday shadows, as though an invisible electric blanket were suspended from the giant trees. The only thing Ray and his captors could do was sit in the shade of their *caletas* and try to stay as cool as possible. One day, lying perfectly still in his shelter, Ray bolted upright. If he were to die that very day, he thought, would he have fulfilled God's purpose for his kidnapping? So far he had stolen moments to talk to the guerrillas one-on-one, as opportunities presented themselves. Still, he knew he had not shared the complete story of God's redemption. If the military ambushed them that very minute, many of the guerrillas would die never having heard about Jesus' death on the cross and the eternal life he offers.

Suddenly Jorge strolled by. He looked at Ray and began ranting in Spanish so fast Ray could barely understand him. *Just angry gibberish,* Ray smirked, then checked himself. *Wouldn't it be just like the Lord to save this guy's soul?* As much as he hated the man's cruelty, Ray knew it would be tragic if Jorge died before he had a chance to hear the truth—not humanistic truth but ultimate, eternal truth. Settling back in a reclined position on his *caleta,* Ray closed his eyes in prayer. *Lord, I don't want to say anything that'll make the guerrillas mad, but I know you want me to tell them about you. Please give me the courage and the opportunity.*

The rest of that afternoon Ray prayed for his captors, thanking God for the friendships he had built over the last few months. Then, suddenly, his face drained of color as another thought entered his head. As friendly as some of them were, if given the order, they would shoot him without hesitation.

Ray and his captors stayed in this location until the rains returned and the camp became mosquito infested. Meanwhile, the days were long, with a constant breeze causing the leaves of the trees to shiver in the ninety-five-degree heat. At night the breeze subsided and the temperature dropped to a comfortable seventy-five degrees. After several dull evenings, Leo complained, "I'm bored!" The others agreed, and Jaime designated a social hour two nights a week.

"Nate, you're in charge of the socials," the commandant said.

Though only nineteen, Nate had seen some combat in his days and was highly regarded by everyone in the camp. Of all the guerrillas so far, he had been the kindest to Ray. He was thoughtful and respectful and Ray liked him, calling him *mi hijo,* or "my son." In the early days of Ray's captivity, when Arnoldo forbade anyone to talk to Ray, Nate frequently ignored the order and chanced opportunities here and there to speak to the hostage. Ray felt sure the letter that was sent to the superior to change out Arnoldo had been written by Nate and signed by the others. During their visits together Nate asked Ray about his family and talked about his own.

"My parents are devout Pentecostals," Nate confided to Ray one afternoon shortly after he'd been taken hostage, when Arnoldo was away. "But I couldn't get into their religion. There were twelve of us kids, and my parents struggled for every dollar. Frequently they didn't even have enough to buy a *bulto* of rice (a going price of five dollars). I couldn't figure out how a God of love could allow us to go so hungry."

Ray sighed. The deprivation this young man must have suffered under those conditions.

"I left school after the first year," Nate continued. "Two of my brothers are in the military now—"[3] His voice trailed off.

"The idea of meeting them in combat, maybe being forced to kill one of your own flesh and blood—" Ray couldn't finish his own sentence. It was too horrific.

Even though he didn't embrace his parents' faith, Nate seemed interested in spiritual things and was open to conversation. Once, Ray had washed his clothes in the stream and had gone into the *llanos* to lay them out on the tall grass to dry. Nate, who was guarding him at the time, accompanied him. For two hours they sat surrounded by the tall grass, talking quietly so the others wouldn't hear.

"So, how is it with your soul?" Ray asked bluntly, his hand raised to his brow in an effort to shield his face from the blazing sun.

By now, Nate knew Ray's interest in him was genuine. Still he shrugged, shirking the question.

"Your soul will live on after you die, Nate. You need to consider where you will spend eternity."

"We all have our destinies," Nate finally responded. "Mine is here. Where my soul ends up . . ." He shrugged again.

"You're right; we all have our destinies, but that doesn't mean we have to stand in front of a speeding truck and say, 'This is my destiny!'" Ray responded. "I believe that God has ultimate control over everything that happens, yet within that control there is a great deal of individual freedom." Nate listened intently but did not answer.

On the night of the first social, Nate introduced a guessing game similar to Truth or Consequences. Whoever was unable to answer a given question had to pay the consequence designated by the one who had asked the question. The game began with Jaime.

"Hmmm. Ramón, can you name three major rivers in the country?"

"That's easy," said Ray. "The Magdalena, the Meta, and the Ariari."

The guerrillas nodded to each other, surprised at his knowledge of their homeland. Next it was Maria's turn.

"José, who sings *"Rey de Despecho"*?

"Don't ask him that!" Jorge sneered. "He knows the answer!"

"I don't care," Maria said. "Go ahead; answer it."

Suddenly José broke out into melodramatic song:

Porque me llaman El Rey de Despecho
Yo nací para atraer el dolor
Es que me duele lo que hace mal hecho
Desde que un amor me pago contracción
Yo otra vez de nuevo estoy enamorado—
Pues mi decisión fué cambiar de mujer . . .
Pero no soy capaz de borrar un recuerdo
Ahora quiero brindar ya que una vez mas
Soy el Rey de Despecho—

Because they call me the King of Rejection
I was born to attract the pain
Now I hurt because of past mistakes
From all this experience I'm wasting away
And now another time I'm in love again—
Well my decision was to get another woman . . .
But I don't have the capacity to erase a memory
Now I want to take the opportunity one more time
I'm the King of Rejection—

Stopping very abruptly, José said, "Darío Gómez." The group groaned.

"Okay, *mi hijo*," Ray said to Nate, "name the capital of Boyacá."

Nate thought for a minute. "I don't know," he finally said.

The guerrillas roared. "Go back to school, little man! Ramón, tell him what he has to do!" Leo cried.

"How about boiling my water in the morning?" Ray answered. The guerrillas laughed again.

Next it was Jorge's turn. "Maria, how many troops are there in a battalion?"

"One hundred and fifty," she snapped. Jorge growled in displeasure that she knew the answer.

"Okay, Ramón, who composed the national anthem?" Linda asked.

"Oh, man . . ." Ray wiped his brow with the palm of his hand. "I've heard the song a million times, but—I don't know."

"Aieee!" the guerrillas howled. "Hey, Linda, what are you going to make him do?" Nate mocked, wanting to get even with the captive.

"Ummm," Linda paused thoughtfully, then her face lit up. "Dance! You have to do a dance!"

The guerrillas howled again, then stood up from their seats and turned toward the hostage, clapping their encouragement.

Ray didn't know how to dance without a partner and wasn't about to invite one of the guerrillas to join him. But he had learned some aerobics and decided that was good enough. Like a spring he jumped into action before the guerrillas, his feet scissoring back and forth and his arms clipping the air above his head. Moving gracefully from side to side, he brought his arms chest high and did some bicep curls, then pushed the air away in front of him with his palms while doing hamstring curls with his legs.

The guerrillas roared until Jaime barked, "Okay, it's eight o'clock. Lights out!" Everyone moaned except Ray, who breathed a sigh of relief. Lying in bed he thought, *No one ever answered the question. . . . Maybe they don't know themselves!* He chuckled.

After several nights even the games became boring, and the guerrillas began to complain again. Suddenly Nate turned to Ray. "Ramón, how about if you lead us in a *culto* [church service]? Maybe you'll convert some of us!" A few of the guerrillas snickered at the prospect; others grumbled. But Nate was in charge, and he'd voiced his decision. Ray looked around at the group of communist disciples sitting before him. What would their reaction be to his Christ-centered message? He always thought he'd be willing to die for the cause of Christ, but was he really? Would this opportunity to share the gospel with them lead to that?

About seven o'clock that evening, with everyone gathered around the lantern-lit table, Ray led the guerrillas in a couple of familiar hymns then asked Leo to read out of the Spanish New Testament Ray carried with him. As Leo stood up to read the psalms Ray had selected, Jorge, who had been standing behind him, jeered, "Now read that loud and clear and try not to laugh!" Then with his usual scowl, Jorge sat down to listen. Leo, self-conscious to be speaking before his peers, faltered over a few words but read until he had finished the assigned passages. Though self-taught, he could read with comprehension and skill. When he was through, Ray took the worn little book from the guerrilla's hands and stood up at the end of the table.

"The Gospel of Matthew, chapter 5 tells us to be perfect, just as our Father in heaven is perfect. But if God alone is perfect, how can we be like him? We are mere humans, who make mistakes and are prone to failure. The Book of Genesis—the first book of the Bible—says that we are made in the image or likeness of God. That's like when a baby is born, you can sometimes look at that baby and say, 'He has brown eyes like his mother,' or 'He's fair skinned like his father.' We have a spirit within us, just as God is a spirit. We are capable of love and forgiveness, just like God. So to be perfect like God, we must allow him to transform us into his likeness, that is, by taking on his personality and character."

Ray hesitated and looked around the table at the blank faces staring back at him. He was not getting through.

"Like the baby. Let's say he lives on a farm with his parents, who grow fruits and vegetables to be sold at the market. Growing up, he will certainly have his own personality, but as he spends time with his mother and father he will begin to pick up their habits and ways of doing things.

Then, when he is mature, he will probably cultivate the soil and sow the seeds at his own farm in the same way his father taught him. If he has any sisters, they will probably cook with the same habits as their mother. You see? We become like those we spend time with. If we spend time with God, we begin to pick up on his traits and characteristics too."

"Do you tell stories like this when you go to the Indian settlements?" Maria asked.

"Well, sometimes, but words like *perfect* are abstract terms, so first we have to learn their language, and then we can translate abstracts into a context they can understand. Take, for instance, the Waorani Indians in Ecuador, where we worked for a couple of years. It took them an entire generation to understand the word *love*. But the biggest challenge is making the initial contact and building trust. With the Waorani, we first made contact with the village by lowering a transmitter basket suspended by a long line from an airplane circling above!" This Ray demonstrated by using a piece of string and a stick for an airplane.

The guerrillas laughed, picturing a basket circling inches above the ground. Ray was happy to have evoked this response from them; at least they had listened!

Two weeks later Nate asked Ray to give another *culto*. Sensing he might not ever have another chance to speak to the guerrillas as a group again, he decided to explain to them God's plan of salvation. He asked for a piece of paper and drew a line divided in two by a chasm. At the bottom of the chasm he drew flames and named the chasm *infierno* (hell). Then he drew a bridge made in the shape of a cross with the words *Jesus Cristo* (Jesus Christ) across the crossbar. On the left of the chasm he drew some stick figures— *hombres y mujeres* (men and women)—and to the right of the chasm he drew a line into *vida eterna* (life eternal), with a sun shining above and the words *Dios Santo* (Holy God). Near the symbols he wrote Scripture references that spoke about what they meant. When the *culto* began, he held up the diagram.

"The Bible says we are all imperfect," Ray began, building on his previous message. Out of the corner of his eye he could see one of the guerrillas, Esther, talking, while Linda giggled. Linda, a large-boned teen with chocolate-colored skin, was an avid reader. She was also quick-witted and could recite all the words to the popular *Vallenato*⁴ songs on the radio as well as many poems and even some Bible verses. She had been silent during the first *culto,* but this time she couldn't stop giggling. Jorge, Nate, and Leo looked at the pair angrily.

"It is our natural inclination to sin, that is, rebel against God and his ways," Ray continued. "Because God is holy and just, he cannot tolerate sin. The Bible teaches that God created the *infierno* for the devil and his angels, but it also makes it clear that the *infierno* will be the eternal destination of those who refuse to believe and obey him. But because he is also a loving God, he created *cielo* (heaven) and provided a way for humans to be forgiven of their sins. As children we are told about the baby Jesus who was born of a virgin on Christmas Day. As a man, Jesus—who was God in the flesh and perfect in every way—died on a cross, then rose from the dead three days later in order that we might have the opportunity to escape a life of sin and eternity in the *infierno.*"

Finally, Linda quit her giggling and spoke up. "It's okay to speak about our imperfections and need for God. But nobody talks to God like we are talking to each other right now, or can know him personally." She leaned into Esther and laughed again, like the idea was preposterous.

"There's a story in the Bible about a man named Nicodemus, who wondered about much the same thing. He went to Jesus at night, looking for answers but not wanting his peers to see him with the carpenter from Nazareth.

What Jesus said astonished him. For humans to know God and have a relationship with him, we must be 'born again.' 'But it's impossible for someone to curl up and crawl back inside his mother's belly,' Nicodemus retorted. But Jesus responded that he wasn't referring to a physical rebirth. For people to know God in the spiritual realm, their spirits must be awakened—they must be 'born again' spiritually. This happens when we acknowledge God as our savior and begin to experience him through reading the Bible and talking to him in prayer."

The guerrillas were silent. Ray wasn't sure if they were thinking about what he had been saying or simply daydreaming about other things. Recalling stories he'd heard from translators returning from Indian villages, of entire families accepting Christ as their savior, he was disappointed that none of his audience showed signs of real interest. But quickly he reminded himself that to do so in this organization might invite strict disciplinary action, rejection by peers, questioning of their dedication to the cause, even accusations of collaboration with the enemy. Only Leo showed any display of emotion. Having studied witchcraft in a country where magic and spiritism are a pervasive way of life, he fidgeted with intense agitation over Ray's words.

Ups and Downs

February to June 1995

> Your sandals shall be iron and bronze; as the days, so shall your strength be.
>
> Deuteronomy 33:25 NKJV

The day after leading his second *culto,* Ray busied himself by installing a headphone jack in a small radio. As his hands worked, his mind turned over the events of the preceding day. The guerrillas responded with seeming apathy to his message, yet knowing that God's Word never returns void, Ray fretted about what kind of yield would eventually come of his efforts. He watched for signs of antagonism among his captors—a look or a superfluous sneer, even neglect. He jumped whenever he heard his name called. Even in his dreams he worried. The previous night he had awakened with a start from a terrifying nightmare: A trap door had opened up in the sky and a dozen guerrillas, heavily armed, stared down at him and laughed. Too afraid to go back to sleep, he stayed awake the rest of the night.

The jack in place, Ray closed up the radio housing and looked at his handiwork. There, before his eyes, were two headphone jacks side by side. "What?" Ray stammered, looking at the radio he held in his hand. *Did I just install a jack where there already was one? Am I losing my mind?*

Ray drew in a deep breath to calm himself. Realizing the irrational bent his mind was taking, he tried to rein in his thoughts. His greatest fear was of becoming mentally or emotionally unstable and doing something rash, like attacking one of the guerrillas, and his thoughts and actions frightened him. Eyes closed, he remembered the prophets who lived in the midst of a similar atmosphere of fear and animosity, yet they counted on God's unfailing presence through whatever encounters came their way. He, too, must not let his imagination run away with him and must lean on his heavenly Father. God had allowed him to safely share the message of salvation with his captors; now he must entrust their reaction, and his fate, to God's trustworthy hands.

Suddenly Jaime walked up, interrupting his thoughts.

"What are the frequency and call letters for Lomalinda?" After Ray supplied the information, the commandant walked away. An hour later he returned.

"I took it upon myself to radio your center and ask about your wife," he blurted out.

Ray sat up in silence, stunned by his captor's courage to take such a bold step without authorization from his superiors.

"They said she's fine. She's in the country of her origin and sends her love."[1]

"Thank you," was all Ray could think to say. As the commandant walked away, Ray sighed. What a relief to know Doris was safe, and what an incredible God he served! Who would have guessed his testimony the previous day would result in personal blessing?

The next day Nate was nowhere to be found. In the evening he returned, and shortly, Ray overheard Jaime chewing out the young guerrilla for carousing with one of the women when he was supposed to be on duty. After being bawled out, Nate sat dejectedly on a broken tree branch. Ray sat down next to him and placed his arm around the guerrilla's shoulders.

"Mi hijo," Ray began, "Ecclesiastes 7:26 says, 'I find more bitter than death the woman who is a snare.' You should be careful not to let the charms of a woman distract you."

"But I need her!"

"Someday, she may be your undoing," Ray concluded.

A few days later, running alongside Ray around the perimeter of the camp as part of the captive's daily exercise routine, Nate broached the subject again.

"You know, I've decided to listen to your advice. These relationships are too hard—they last only until one of us is transferred to another unit."

"Well, Nate, the Lord told me to talk to you about your relationship, so that's why I did it. I care about what happens to you."

Ray and his guard had stopped jogging and were catching their breath. Abruptly, Nate exclaimed, "I can see you were doing a good work here in Colombia; you didn't deserve to be kidnapped." Just then Jaime passed by and gave them a disturbing look. The two men began jogging again in silence, but Ray wondered if the commandant had overheard them.

Within a week, Nate was changed out of the unit. Before he left Ray prayed with him, then never saw him again. Nor was he invited to lead another *culto.* For days he tried to convince himself the young man could have been transferred for any number of reasons, but he couldn't shake the thought that it was because the guerrilla had encouraged him to share his faith, and listened to his advice. He felt awful. From that moment on, Ray vowed not to interfere with the personal affairs of any of his captors. He didn't want to be perceived as a pesky meddler, nor did he want to cause trouble. "Conduct yourselves in a manner worthy of the gospel of Christ" (Phil. 1:27), he reminded himself, and of course that meant in the context of the surrounding culture.

But following his own advice proved difficult. One of the young women fairly new to the camp, Lilly, constantly walked around moaning over her assignment to guard Ray. She wished his organization would just pay the ransom so she could get back to her boyfriend in another unit. Then, a previous boyfriend arrived in camp and she latched on to him.

One day Lilly asked Ray to cut her hair. As he snipped at the guerrilla's long mane, he asked, "Lilly, have you ever read the Bible?"

"When I was little."

"There's a story in it about Jesus meeting a woman at a well outside her town. Jesus had never met her before but knew her past—that she had had five husbands and the man she was then living with was not her husband. He knew she was looking for meaning in her life but looking in all the wrong places."

Lilly sat silently for a moment, then asked, "So what happened?"

Ray had finished with her hair and sat down on the bench beside her. "Jesus told her where to find the meaning she was searching for." He opened the green Spanish New Testament and, turning to John 4, read the story to her.

"This living water, does it have to do with the picture you drew?"

Ray pulled out his bridge illustration and helped Lilly find each of the Bible verses corresponding to the concepts on the paper. She read the verses, rubbing her abdomen occasionally.

Ray pointed to her stomach. "Is something wrong?"

"I had surgery on my ovaries a while ago, but something's not right. I hurt."

"You're too young for that kind of surgery."

Lilly nodded her head.

The next day she returned and asked to read the same story again, then thanked Ray. A few days later a group of the guerrillas stood about complaining. Bored, they blamed Ray for the monotony in their lives. Lilly passed by and heard them haranguing the captive. "Cases like this don't help our cause any, you know," she said, pointing to Ray. "It's our fault he's here!"

Within a few days, Lilly left. The guerrillas said she had gone to see a doctor and would be fine, but she never returned.

As the weeks passed, Ray and Jaime became better acquainted. Although the commandant could be harsh and unforgiving with the guerrillas, he showed kindness to the captive. One of the hardest things for Ray to deal with was the constant unknown factor of moving from camp to camp. Finding himself in the commandant's good graces, he asked that he be told in advance when they planned to move. The commandant honored his request. Sometimes he even tried to arrange a horse or mule for Ray to ride on. And, like Omar before him, he lent Ray his radio to listen to Christian programming.

One particular Sunday in May, as rain poured from the sky and slapped against the plastic roofing of his *caleta,* Ray sat with his ear to the radio listening to the opening music of a worship program, singing along and allowing the strains of a favorite hymn to lift his spirits:

> There's not a friend like the lowly Jesus,
> No, not one! no, not one!
> None else could heal all our soul's diseases,
> No, not one! no, not one!
>
> No friend like Him is so high and holy,
> No, not one! no, not one!

And yet no friend is so meek and lowly,
No, not one! no, not one!

There's not an hour that He is not near us,
No, not one! no, not one!
No night so dark but His love can cheer us,
No, not one! no, not one!

Did ever saint find this Friend forsake him?
No, not one! no, not one!
Or sinner find that He would not take him?
No, not one! no, not one!

Was e'er a gift like the Savior given?
No, not one! no, not one!
Will He refuse us a home in heaven?
No, not one! no, not one!

Following the hymn, the announcer prayed, thanking God for his many blessings and encouraging listeners not to forget that "every good gift and every perfect gift is from above, and comes down from the Father of lights, with whom there is no variation or shadow of turning" (James 1:17 NKJV). At the end of the prayer, Ray added his own thank you for the radio he listened to. Suddenly a thought dawned on him. Hadn't Jaime gone out of his way on many occasions to demonstrate kindness? Was it possible God had Ray's captivity in mind when, years ago, he showed this man kindness and hospitality in his own home? An image of God standing on a forty-foot ladder overlooking a labyrinth entered Ray's mind. From that vantage point, God could see the end of Ray's life from the beginning, as well as every step along the way, and could prepare the way ahead of him. All he needed to do was listen to God and follow instructions.

Later that afternoon, Ray was sitting in his *caleta* trying to keep cool and avoid the mosquitoes when he heard a

140

noise coming from behind him in the woods. The clamor grew louder and Ray became nervous. Who or what was in the woods approaching their camp? Suddenly a *lapa*[2] broke through a thicket of small trees and thundered through their midst. The guerrillas burst into action—what a delicacy if they could catch it! A handful of the guerrillas tried to herd the animal into a corner, where another guerrilla waited with a shovel ready to kill it. Just as suddenly as the *lapa* had run into the camp, four dogs came crashing through the woods chasing after it. The *lapa* shot off toward the riverbank where it darted into a *gurri*[3] hole, the dogs hot on its trail. One of the dogs dashed into the hole after it. Even with the dogs barking, the guerrillas could hear the brawl down in the hole and knew the dog had the animal by the tail.

Suddenly a hunter broke into the guerrilla camp.

"Quick, hide yourself!" José, who was in charge while Jaime was away, ordered the captive. Ray took the newspaper he was reading, lay down, and put it over his face.

The hunter stopped in the middle of the camp and stared at José, who was standing, hands on hips, in between two *caletas*. "You can't come through here; you have to go around."

"But the *lapa*—" the hunter argued.

"Forget the *lapa*. Call off your dogs and leave!" José boomed.

The hunter whistled for his dogs, who immediately ran after their master. To the guerrillas' aggravation, the dog in the hole retreated without the *lapa*. Now what were they to do? Bringing a shovel from camp, they dug straight down into the soft riverbank until they connected with the *gurri* tunnel. There, just a few feet down the hole, was the *lapa*, dead, with its hindquarters eaten by the dog. That night they had the tastiest meal Ray had ever eaten.

The next day—having noted all the *gurri* holes the day before—the guerrillas decided to go hunting for the armored creatures whose soft underbellies tasted like chicken when baked. With a dog in tow, they wandered along the banks of the river, waiting for the dog to indicate a hole with a fresh scent. Then they shoved a long, flexible stick into the hole to determine the direction of the tunnel and began digging every few feet along its path. Finally, they caught a glimpse of a *gurri's* tail—he was on the run! Quickly they dug and dug, eventually ending up with a trench three feet deep and twenty feet long, but still no *gurri*. As a last resort they poured water down the trench trying to flush the *gurri* out of the tunnel he was burrowing.

Watching this spectacle from a distance, Ray laughed. "The *gurri* won, didn't he?"

"For today; tomorrow we'll get him," Abel, one of the guerrillas, said. Sometimes Abel said and did the strangest things, and Ray worried that he wasn't quite right in the head. He hated the thought of the man carrying a firearm and stayed well out of his way.

The next day the guerrillas took a different tack. They mounted a shotgun across the top of two stakes and attached a wire to the trigger. Then they strung the wire across the path leading between two active *gurri* holes. Evening came and the sky darkened. The guerrillas sat perfectly still, listening for the distinct noise of the *gurris* as they came out of their burrows and rambled through the underbrush for food. Hearing the rustle of the ground cover, they carefully approached the rigged holes. Suddenly the shotgun blasted. The guerrillas flashed their lights in the direction of the gun and saw a dead *gurri* lying on the ground.

"Sure beats hitting it over the head with a shovel," Abel remarked.

On May 25, Ray sat huddled inside his shelter while a light drizzle fell outside. Due to the weather the entire camp had been cooped up in their quarters for hours. After lunch,

Abel sidled up to Ray's *caleta*. "Do you want to watch a *telenovela?*"[4] the guerrilla asked.

"Oh, sure." Ray hated soap operas—calling them *telementiras* (TV lies)—but the guerrillas could not watch the shows unless he wanted to, and since everyone was bored, he decided to humor them. In a moment everyone was gathered around Jaime's TV set, while the commandant answered a call on the radio.

Suddenly, Jaime ran toward the cluster of men and women. "Shut the TV off! The military is headed our way!"

After a quick meeting with the others, Jaime hurried over to Ray's *caleta* and told him to pack up—they would be heading out after sundown. An hour later they heard the beating of helicopter propellers in the distance.

"Get moving, *now!*" the commandant yelled.

For ten minutes the guerrillas were a blur of activity as they began feverishly tearing the camp apart, leaving no trace of their presence. They dismantled the furniture—tables, chairs, *caletas*—and strewed the wood about haphazardly. Ray did his part by stripping the netting off his bed of sticks and cleaving the wooden joints apart, then throwing all his belongings into his backpack. Soon the choppers could be seen emerging from the clouds.

"Everyone down!" Jaime called out, then skidded into a thicket. As the entire camp lay motionless under bushes and clusters of trees, they watched as the choppers passed by. Slowly the noise of the propellers grew fainter and everyone began to stir.

"We were lucky; that was close," Jaime said, standing up and looking into the distance after the row of retreating helicopters.

Rising slowly from the ground, Ray felt his heart pounding wildly in his chest. In the frenzy of the last few minutes he hadn't realized how frightened he was. He walked over to a nearby felled tree branch and sat for a moment, giving his heart a chance to recover and thanking God for his protection. Suddenly a passage of Scripture he'd read just days before popped into his head. It was the story of the apostle Paul's voyage to Rome and his shipwreck at sea. "Do not be afraid, Paul. You must stand trial before Caesar; and God has graciously given you the lives of all who sail with you" (Acts 27:24). Ray didn't know who the "Caesar" might be in his life, but he knew God was telling him that no harm would come to any in his party as long as he was in captivity.

That night, after all danger of air raid had passed, Ray and his captors trudged single file through what had turned into a downpour, past jungle and *llanos,* back toward the river where they had camped in December. It was a nice campsite and, with the recent rains, the river would be high enough to sustain them. In the early morning light, Ray saw that a *caleta* had already been prepared for him. He crawled in and changed out of his soaking uniform into dry clothes, then followed orders to stay put while the others prepared the camp. As he lay reading his Bible, Leo came up and sat on the corner of his *caleta.* Leo liked conversing, even to himself sometimes. Half the time it sounded to Ray like nonsense, and he ignored him.

"You looked surprised to see a *caleta* waiting here for you. Didn't you know the commandant had sent Tony ahead to build it?"

"No, I didn't know that, Leo."

"He's black, you know."

"I've noticed that."

"He's good at tying up the mosquitoes at night because he's camouflaged—the bugs can't see him."

Ray looked at the guerrilla and sighed. Leo sat quietly for several minutes, watching a horsefly as it buzzed around and landed on his leg.[5] He slowly snuck his hand up behind the bug and caught its wings between his fingers. Taking a bottle of super glue from his shirt pocket, he dropped a bit of the glue on the insect's wings, blew them dry, then released the bug.

"Tell me about the *gringo* girls at Lomalinda. I've seen some of them; they're very pretty."

"Ah, Leo, *usted no tiene arreglo*" ("you're beyond repair")! Several of the other guerrillas, including Jaime, overheard the hostage say this and laughed. Leo got up in a huff and walked away.

"It's true," Jaime said to Ray out of earshot of the others. Ray chuckled, then was suddenly silenced by a verse that exploded in his mind: "Do not call anything impure that God has made clean" (Acts 10:15) . . . or can make clean! Immediately Ray felt bad. Said half in jest, the statement was uncalled for and could only harm his relationship with this guerrilla who was so spiritually needy. Ray whispered a prayer of repentance for making fun at the expense of his captors. They—just like the saints in heaven—were created in God's image and were deserving of God's love and care.

Early the following morning they heard helicopters off in the distance, in the direction of the area they had just evacuated. Ray spent the rest of the morning watching the guerrillas complete the task of turning the small trees surrounding the camp into furniture. As the hours passed, his skin began to itch and burn about his waist, inside his elbows, and on the backs of his knees. Running his fingers over those areas, Ray felt welts raising up on his skin. Chiggers! For the next two weeks he suffered with the boils caused by the blood-sucking larvae. Only some borrowed red nail polish helped relieve the burning. Spotted with dots, he looked as though he had chicken pox.

A few days after the arrival of June, one of the guerrillas brought a rash of electronic equipment to Ray for repair: televisions, clock radios, boom boxes, cassette recorders. The items came from the locals in the area, and in exchange

145

for the repair work, the guerrillas received chickens. Ray thanked his captors for the work; it kept him busy and gave him something to listen to.

On June 16, Jaime approached Ray as he worked on a radio. "You need to write a letter to your wife."

Bewildered at the request, Ray happily obliged. He began the letter with the heading, "443 days [in captivity], letter number 42."

Ever since his first day in the guerrilla camp, Jorge had been a source of contention with his vulgar language and harsh treatment. As new recruits entered the camp, his abusive behavior rubbed off on some of them, and currently three other guerrillas treated the hostage as cruelly as Jorge. One, a teenager, had grown up in Puerto Lleras and knew Ray from the times Ray had come to school delivering notebooks. Knowing his captors read his letters, Ray decided to take a bold step to try and rid himself of these four men. After the usual greetings, he wrote, "I'm nervous a lot, and when I'm nervous I don't need someone bothering me. These guys are bothering me," he said, naming the four guerrillas. Within a week the four men were rounded up and ordered to another unit. "Well, they're going to send in some *really* good replacements now!" Jorge sneered at Ray as he passed by on his way out of camp. Ray began to worry—what if the next ones are worse than these four?

"Come on, Ramón, let's get some sun," Tony said to the captive. Ray had fixed his tape recorder a few months before, and the guerrilla had treated the captive kindly ever since. After they entered a clearing, Tony continued. "What grief we've caused you, to have to put up with these guys. You remember the Coca-Cola that was stolen from my *caleta* a few months ago? I think it was either Jorge or one of his cohorts who did it. We're getting people into the organization who are uneducated and they act like this. The only thing we can do is change them out."

Listening to the guerrilla talk, Ray prayed about the replacements, that they would not be like Jorge. When they returned to camp, a couple of new men had already arrived, one being a young man named Pablo. When he saw Ray, he amiably walked up to the captive and shook his hand.

On the nineteenth of the month, one of the guerrillas brought a radio cassette player to Ray saying the tape deck didn't work. Ray cleaned and soldered and rewired the gadget all morning. Finally, after several tries, he got the tape player working again. With the guerrillas standing around, he turned on the radio to be sure it was functioning properly. As he did so, the disc jockey interrupted the music with a breaking news story about the deaths of two American missionaries from New Tribes Mission—Steve Welsh and Tim Van Dyke—who had been kidnapped by guerrillas from Villavicencio ten weeks before Ray's abduction. Their bodies had been found in the midst of a guerrilla camp after a skirmish between their captors and the military, in which they had been caught in the cross fire.

After the initial announcement, Teddy Tournbaum, director of the Colombian Red Cross in the state of Meta, came on the radio, making comments about the two missionaries who'd been killed. He said he was going to check on the welfare of the other foreigners being held hostage in Meta.

Ray's eyes widened as the broadcast continued. "We didn't kill them—we don't kill prisoners!" Luis, who had recently returned to camp after a hernia operation, said.

Three days later Jaime asked Ray to come over to his *caleta*. "You have a message from the front," he said. "The two *norteamericanos* were killed when the military came into the camp shooting at anything standing on two legs. They shot those two fellows."

"Jaime, do you believe that?" Ray said.

"*Sí,*" Jaime said. "We don't kill prisoners."

147

Ray thanked him and walked away. He wanted to believe him, but the news raised many unanswered questions. It seemed as though in his situation the guerrillas took every precaution to protect him from harm, moving whenever they discovered the military was near. He'd begun to trust them. Yet he'd heard too many stories about hostages being killed after a negotiation gone awry to dismiss the nagging doubts that persisted in his mind, and this news added fresh fodder to that smoldering flame. Why hadn't the other guerrillas kept Tim and Steve out of danger, as his captors did for him? Is it possible they had truly been caught off guard? Or had they killed the men, using the military attack as a cover?

And what did this mean for him?

Keep trusting the Lord and in him alone.

Airdrop

February 1995

New Year's came and went in silence. Having had high hopes that the flyer distribution in Puerto Lleras and radio broadcast throughout the *llanos* would yield renewed contact with Ray's captors, by February 1995, the crisis committee was deeply concerned. Something had to be done to grab the guerrillas' attention. They decided to try a leaflet drop from the air over the area west and south of Lomalinda. The guerrillas controlled much of that territory; surely they would find a copy. Plus, the people of the region would be reminded once more of Ray.

Appealing to the sentiments of the Colombian people, the leaflet said:

Attention Colombian People:

Mrs. Clarice Rising, the dearly loved mother of Ray Rising, now eighty-nine years old, has just spent Christmas without the comfort of having any news about her son. Could it be that this poor woman will have to end her few days remaining to her alone, with her sight failing, with a heart in anguish, knowing nothing about her son Ray?

We appeal with all our heart to the conscience of the Colombian people, to help bring to pass the last wish to this valiant widow of seeing her dear son one more time, or at least receiving some message from him, telling how he is.

On February 23, Dean Albany piloted a Helio Courier airplane away from the Lomalinda airstrip. While he flew low over the little villages and towns in the region, George Kavanaugh and Brian Gray tossed handfuls of the leaflets out the window and watched them disperse and flutter to the ground.

Several days passed in silence. Early one morning near the end of the month, Lomalinda received a strange radio communication from a guerrilla claiming to be holding the captive and asking questions about Doris. Then, very abruptly, the guerrilla ended the connection before the crisis committee could ask about reopening negotiations. They were no further along than they were before, but at least there was one glimmer of hope on the horizon that Ray was yet alive.

Alive and Well

May to June 1995

May arrived—nine months since the last real communication from the guerrillas—yet rumors persisted that Ray had been killed. With no concrete evidence to support the hearsay, the committee clung to the hope that it was erroneous. Still, an underlying current of uncertainty weighed heavily on everyone's mind.

About this time, Ricardo (not his real name) approached the crisis team, offering to deliver a letter to the guerrillas requesting that they reinstate negotiations. By this time George Kavanaugh had departed for furlough, and Mark Litz now headed up the crisis team. After Mark had settled into his new post, a letter was composed and sent, followed by more waiting.

On June 20, the crisis team heard a report, regarding a different hostage case, that shook them to the core. Timothy Van Dyke and Steve Welsh, two missionaries from New Tribes Mission who had been kidnapped in Villavicencio just ten weeks prior to Ray's abduction, were dead—killed in cross fire between the military and the guerrilla unit holding them. Mark and many others wept over the news, in compassion for the wives and families of these two men, and in despair, wondering what it might mean for their crisis. If prayer is the incense that perfumes God's throne, it can only be imagined what a fragrance must have filled heaven that day.

In contrast to the previous day's pain, June 21 brought wonderful news: Ray was alive! Brian Gray called up Mark on the telephone, urging him to hurry over. Ricardo had returned with a reply from Ray's captors! Included in the message from the guerrillas was a handwritten note from Ray dated June 16.[6] The drought in communication appeared to be over.

8

Justice and Mercy

June to November 1995

> He has shown you, O man, what is good; and what does the
> LORD require of you but to do justly, to love mercy, and to
> walk humbly with your God?
>
> > Micah 6:8 NKJV

The rest of June dragged by uneventfully, yet with
the news of the New Tribes men's deaths looming in his
thoughts, Ray suffered bouts of depression. Making matters worse was Luis's handling of the hostage after returning from his operation. In his absence, Ray had grown used
to walking anywhere he wanted and talking to anyone he
pleased in the camp. Now the guerrilla began to regulate
the captive's every move as he had done previously. This
time, though, Ray realized Luis's treatment was his own
idea and not the commandant's, and Ray was determined
not to let the guerrilla control him. But he also knew he
needed to be careful how he dealt with the situation, as the
Lord had warned him recently in Scripture to be on his
guard.[1]

After breakfast one day in a new campsite, Luis began ranting to Ray about some rules he'd concocted.

"I don't agree with these rules of yours," Ray said. "Maybe it's time we talked with the commandant about them." Seeing Tony standing nearby, Ray went over to him and explained the problem. Tony had the same temperament as Luis, and the two didn't get along. Yet Tony was better respected among the guerrillas, and Ray knew he would be an asset to his cause.

"Well, let's see what Jaime has to say," Tony replied loud enough for Luis to hear.

"No . . . it's okay, no problem . . ." Luis said, backing down. For a while after that he left Ray alone but continued to harass the others, picking at their sloppy appearance and the way they fulfilled their role while on guard duty.

July 1 dawned hot, humid, and rainy, dampening Ray's spirits even more than usual. Over a year had passed since his captivity began, and he saw no end in sight. Downhearted, he wrote a letter to the commander of the front that was holding him, pleading for his freedom. He did not know how the letter would be received, but he gave it to Jaime anyway. *I have plenty of time and nothing to lose,* he thought.

That night an overcast sky held in the hot, moist air, exaggerating the silence except for the occasional croaking of frogs near the water. Suddenly, Ray awoke from a fitful sleep to the sound of a nearby snore. He sat up, perfectly still, and listened carefully to the noises of the night. There it was again! An unmistakable snore, coming from the direction of the guard chair. Was it possible his guard had fallen asleep? He sat there for several minutes, listening to the rhythmic noise of the guard's heavy breathing, and prayed fervently. Slowly, carefully, he rose from his *caleta,* lifted the mosquito netting, and crept toward the guard. Standing within a few feet of the guerrilla, Ray shone his flashlight on him. The guerrilla sat with his head in his lap and his arms dangling loosely over each end of his rifle so that Ray couldn't tell who it was.

The hostage walked to the edge of camp and hesitated. "Lord, is this my opportunity to escape?" he whispered under his breath. He turned around and shone the light again on the guerrilla, who was sleeping soundly. God's response came immediately. *Wait on the Lord, be of good courage and he shall strengthen your heart. Wait, I say, on the Lord.*

Ray sighed, remembering God's promise to him of freedom from Psalm 146. The Lord would free the captive in his own time and way, and this was not it. With a heavy heart but knowing he was doing the right thing, he went over to José's *caleta*.

"José—"

José jerked into consciousness and turned on his flashlight, shining it in Ray's face.

"The guard's snoring is keeping me awake."

Ray returned to his *caleta* while José woke up the guard, who turned out to be a twenty-year-old named Felipe. The following day, José explained what had happened to the commandant. A habitual liar, Felipe tried to make excuses for the incident, but finally Jaime interrupted him and ordered him to dig new sanitation and garbage holes the rest of the day.

Curiously, their current campsite was devoid of any wildlife—birds, monkeys, *gurris,* even rats. Ray thought that very unusual for the jungle but soon discovered empty bags of pesticides in the surrounding coca fields and wondered if that accounted for the disparity. After days with no meat and tired of his starchy diet, Leo decided to find a local farmer and bring back a chicken. After several hours he returned to camp—barefoot, with a chicken slung across his back and talking a hundred miles an hour. Leo had a habit of running his words together, and Ray always had a hard time understanding him, but this time the captive couldn't comprehend a word he was saying.

"Now slow down, Leo. Speak good Spanish so I can understand you," Ray said.

"I was crossing a stream, holding the chicken and my revolver in one hand and my boots in the other . . . the water was up to my chest. As I got close to the other side of the stream, I saw in some branches overhanging the water two huge anacondas[2] curled up and looking at me! So I dropped my boots and got out of there!"

Ray looked down at the guerrilla's bare feet and chuckled. "Looks like your feet are about the same size as mine. Do you want to borrow my rubber boots until you can replace yours?" Leo looked flabbergasted at Ray's offer. Without his rubber boots, the hostage would have to wear his leather cowboy boots, which weren't much good in the jungle. All the same, Leo accepted Ray's proposal.

As Leo took Ray's rubber boots, Luis jeered at his comrade's thoughtlessness: "Why didn't you just shoot the snakes!"

Later that evening, Luis was guarding Ray when the hostage asked if he could watch television with the others in Jaime's *caleta,* as the commandant had built a large thatched roof over his shelter to accommodate everyone. Luis refused his request, so Ray lay in his *caleta* the entire evening.

The following morning, one of the girls, Adriana, approached Ray as he did his morning devotions. Eighteen years old, she treated the hostage with kindness and dignity, always asking him what he wanted to eat (even though she disliked cooking) and doing her best to prepare things to his taste.

"Don Ramón, what would you like for lunch today?" she asked.

"Do you have any more of those little canned Vienna sausages?"

"Maybe when our next supply comes in. How about some *tortas*[3] or fried potatoes and fruit juice?"

"Whatever you come up with will be fine," Ray said.

"Why didn't you watch TV with us last night?" the young woman asked.

"Because Luis wouldn't let me," Ray replied.

Adriana's hazel eyes grew dark as she scowled. Without a word, she stomped off to find Jaime. The two spoke for a minute, then she went about her duties.

That evening, with Luis in the guard's chair again, Adriana strode up to Ray's *caleta*. Ignoring the guerrilla, she spoke directly to Ray.

"Ramón, put your boots on; you're going to watch TV with me tonight."

Luis jumped up from the chair. "What's he going to do that for?" he raged.

"To enjoy it!" Adriana retorted. Ray put on his leather boots and watched shows into the evening with the others, leaving Luis in the guard chair all by himself.

The next morning, before Luis had been relieved of his shift, Ray left his *caleta* and asked another guerrilla for some solder for a repair job he expected to do that day. Luis fumed that his charge had left his shelter and spoken without permission but didn't say anything until Felipe came on duty. In customary fashion, the former guard updated the relieving guerrilla about anything noteworthy; at that time, Luis erupted in a tirade of complaints to his comrade, who later told Ray.

"This problem's gotten out of hand. I think it's time to tell Jaime," Ray said, desperate for a resolution.

Like the others, Felipe was tired of Luis's derision. "Do you want me to get the commandant for you?" he quickly offered.

As Jaime passed by, Felipe beckoned him over to Ray's *caleta,* where the captive explained the trouble.

"He yanks me around like a dog on the end of a leash," Ray told the commandant. "I know I'm a prisoner, but I've never given you any trouble, and I don't think I deserve being treated like this. Sometimes I'm afraid Luis is going to shoot me!"

"Oh, no, he won't do that because he knows he'll get the same thing," Jaime replied, knowing Luis was listening. Without a word to his fellow guerrilla, the commandant walked away. Ray looked at Luis's face, red and full of rage, and wondered if he'd done the right thing. Luis loved to brag about the people he'd killed or mutilated over the years, and Ray didn't want to fall victim to the guerrilla's wrath.

On the evening of July 11, Ray, Merci, and the commandant were sitting around the commandant's television when a breaking news story about the Cali drug cartel interrupted the program they were watching. In recent weeks three of the cartel's leaders—Gilberto Rodriguez Orejuela, Henry "The Scorpion" Loaiza Ceballos, and Victor Patiño—had been arrested or turned themselves in. Now, according to the news announcer, the mastermind behind the Cali cartel, José Santacruz Londoño, was behind bars as well:

> "Tonight, José Santacruz Londoño, architect of the Cali cartel, is behind bars in a Bogotá jail. Santacruz was flushed out of his hometown early last month by an elite government strike force and has been on the run since. But this evening, two police officers spotted the druglord dining with three business associates in Carbon de Palo, a reputed favorite steak house of the kingpin. 'He was considerably heavier than our photographs,' said General Rosso José Serrano Cadena, chief of the Colombian National Police. Nevertheless, upon sighting Santacruz, otherwise known as 'El Gordo' [The Fat One], the officers notified Serrano. Realizing the restaurant was only blocks away from his personal residence, Serrano ordered

his own bodyguards to make the arrest. 'Santacruz was in a very shocked state,' Serrano said.

"Shortly after Santacruz's arrest, another cartel leader, Phanor Arizabaleta Arzayuz, turned himself in. Suspected of having some connection to the murder of a police intelligence officer, Arizabaleta claims he is innocent of any wrong-doing and only turned himself in to clear his reputation.

"I repeat, this evening, druglords Santacruz and Ariza-baleta are behind bars in Bogotá."

Stunned, Merci leaned into Jaime's chest. "Did you hear that?"

"*Sí,*" the commandant replied.

"What's going to happen now?"

Jaime only shook his head.

The next morning Merci was crying, afraid for herself. Victor, the medic, was in camp that day and came over to talk to her, but she would not be consoled, so he went about his business. Then Ray approached the guerrilla.

"You know, Merci, God has promised me that nothing bad will happen to any of you as long as I'm here in captivity."

"What about after that? What will happen then?" she sobbed.

"What you're involved in is very dangerous," Ray agreed. After a moment's hesitation, he went on. "I'll tell you something. On May 21, I was listening to some Christian programs on the radio. Two separate times that day I heard the message, *victoria a la justicia* [victory to justice]. Then later in the evening, in my own devotions, I read Matthew 12:20: 'A bruised reed he will not break, and a smoldering wick he will not snuff out, till he leads justice to victory.'"

Ray opened up his Bible and showed the passage to the guerrilla, who took the book into her own hands and read the verse aloud.

159

"That means someday all the wrongdoers in the world will be held accountable for what they've done," Ray continued. "Right now, many people are doing evil things, like these druglords, thinking they're getting away with it. But God knows and is bringing them to justice."

When Ray had finished sharing his thoughts with Merci, she nodded her head very seriously. "Thank you, Don Ramón," she said, drying her eyes.

Two weeks later, on July 31, Jaime took Ray aside and showed him a letter written on June 29 to the guerrilla commander and signed by the SIL crisis committee. The letter indicated a concern for Ray's welfare and expressed a desire to resume communications with his captors. After Ray had finished reading the letter, Jaime folded it and stuffed it into his pocket.

"We're trying to work things out," Jaime said, attempting to console the captive after his recent letter to the front commander. "Try to be patient."

During September and early October, military activity in the area and weekly surveillance planes flying low overhead kept the guerrilla camp on the move, and Ray had to be prepared to run on a moment's notice. In the midst of this, on October 15, Jaime said good-bye to the hostage and was replaced by Omar, who had spent the previous nine months in another unit. Shortly after Omar arrived, Ray was standing in a clearing near a felled tree, admiring the blue sky and sunshine,[4] when a surveillance plane flew directly overhead, then banked sharply to the left.

"We've been discovered. Let's get out of here!" Omar yelled. A couple of the guerrillas had already been preparing another campsite, so at four o'clock the next morning Ray and his captors set out. The ground was soggy from a heavy rain earlier that night, and the line of uniformed men and women moved sluggishly through the tangled underbrush. After several hours of slow going they came to a river, swollen, swift, and impassable. Without a canoe there was no way across, so the unit set up a makeshift camp on the riverbank and waited for the water to retreat. After three days they moved on. Finally, they arrived at their destination, but even with the military operations further away, Omar felt uncomfortable and decided to move to a completely different area. After extensive preparations, they set out across the backwoods heading east with Ray riding on the back of a mule. After a full day's journey they crested a hill; in the valley below them lay an abandoned farmhouse.

"We'll sleep there for the night," Omar said.

Excited about the prospect of sleeping with a roof over his head, Ray kicked the mule, but the animal wouldn't budge.

"Hiyaa!" Ray yelled, digging his heels into the mule's ribs, but still the animal balked. The guerrillas laughed—it looked like a scene from a cartoon! Finally, Omar pulled the animal by the reins, and reluctantly the mule ambled down the hill. After a good night's sleep and another long day of travel, they pitched their rain ponchos under a clear sky on top of a hill overlooking a ranch. Lying under the stars for the first time in over a year, Ray reminisced about camping trips with the Boys' Brigade and fell asleep with his sons' names on his lips.

The next three days they alternated between sleeping during the day and traveling at night, and traveling during the day and sleeping at night. On the fifth day, having left the mule behind, Ray was walking down a hill when he stepped into a hole covered with a layer of humus and distended his right knee. For the rest of that day and the next, he hobbled along with a walking stick through woods and fields of coca plants. While heading through one such field, the travelers came across a group of young people picking coca leaves and putting them on a sheet of black plastic on the ground. *They look like city folks. I wonder if any of them*

161

have heard of me? Ray thought. One of the men was a heavy-set fellow with long, blond, curly hair. As Ray and Abel passed within twenty feet of him, Ray looked over at his guard, then winked at the man a couple of times.

At the end of the field they came to a fence. The other guerrillas hurdled the wooden crossbars first, followed by Abel, who laid his twelve-gauge pump shotgun against one of the posts before crawling over. He walked ahead several yards, then turned and waited for Ray to cross over. Ray approached the fence and looked at the gun. His mind went into high gear—surrounded by guerrillas, he couldn't get away with taking the gun, but he could have a little fun. He passed over the fence and walked ahead of Abel. After walking one hundred feet with the guard on his heels, he turned and faced him.

"Abel, how are we going to hunt *gurris* without a gun?"

"Oh, you noticed that, huh?" the guerrilla said sheepishly. Calling one of the others to keep an eye on Ray, he ran back and retrieved his gun from the fence post.

That evening everyone gave Abel a hard time, especially the captive. "Poor Abel, all shook up over those nice-looking girls working in the field! We'll have to sanction him, won't we?" he said. The others agreed and roared with laughter.

Curled up in his rain poncho that night under the stars, Ray thought over the events of the day and wondered what would come of his signal to the blond-haired man. He was sure the man had noticed—would he tell anyone what he'd seen? The next morning he found out. As dawn broke, Omar strode into the improvised camp and confronted the hostage.

"One of the field workers told me you were signaling him yesterday with a wink. Were you?"

"Signaling him? No, I . . . I was saluting him. He looked American, and in our culture a wink is a salute. That's all." Normally a very truthful man, Ray wondered if his face gave him away, but the commandant seemed satisfied with his response.

"He wanted to know who you were. I told him you were a medical doctor traveling with us."

After six days of trekking east, they arrived at a new camp-site where telltale signs indicated that guerrillas had been there before. After a night's rest they began to set up camp but were interrupted mid-morning by bombers flying directly overhead, followed by troop-carrying helicopters. Obviously they couldn't stay there! Tired of the uncertainty of constant movement, everyone packed up and left, this time finding a quiet, secluded location near a stream. There was no indication anyone had been there before, which meant more preparation but less chance of surveillance. Within a few days, with no military interruption, they had settled into their new home.

With camp in order, Ray wondered if negotiations were continuing for his release. He knew there had been at least some contact with the crisis committee back in July and had hoped he might be home for Christmas. Now, further away from civilization than ever and with no word from the commandant, he began to give up hope of seeing his family any time soon. Again, boredom and intense loneliness set in. Sure, he was surrounded by people at all times and in fact had no privacy whatsoever, but none of the guerrillas shared his innermost thoughts and feelings and he felt isolated and depressed.

One morning, as Ray lay in his *caleta* after morning devotions, he caught sight of a newcomer arriving in camp, a very attractive young woman with dark hair and skin. Looking very confident, she strolled around the camp greeting everyone. Finally, she came within fifteen feet of Ray's *caleta* and stopped, staring in his direction. Ray sat up and looked at her; she continued staring, with the corners of her lips turned up in a slight smile.

"Come over here," Ray beckoned, swinging his legs over the side of his *caleta*. The woman brushed her long hair away from her shoulders, then sauntered up to the captive.

"My name is Ramón. I'm friends with everyone here; please don't be afraid of me or hate me," the hostage said, knowing many guerrillas harbor a deep disdain for Americans.

"Oh, no, I wouldn't do that! My name is Elise." She held out her hand to Ray, who shook it gently.

For the next several days Elise went about her duties like everyone else, but each time she passed Ray's shelter she turned her head in his direction and stared at him. With each passing day, Ray enjoyed her company and looked forward to their chats on the edge of his *caleta*.

One day as the captive thought about his new friend, God spoke to him from 1 Peter 2:11–12. "Dear friends, I urge you, as aliens and strangers in the world, to abstain from sinful desires, which war against your soul. Live such good lives among the pagans that, though they accuse you of doing wrong, they may see your good deeds and glorify God on the day he visits us." Ray felt the words piercing his heart and soul and hung his head in repentant sorrow. *I'm sorry, Lord. I know I've sinned and hurt you deeply. You're all I need, even now. Please protect me from myself, and forgive me.* The following day he heard Dr. Joe Stowell on the radio talking about adultery and similar types of temptations. "Don't go out of your fortress to pick the daisies," Stowell concluded. *Wow,* Ray thought. *The Lord has a way of getting his point across.* The captive spent the rest of the day praising God for his love and faithfulness, displayed through his constant care and even through his chastisement.

After several days of reining in his thoughts, Ray contemplated the potential results of wrongdoing had God not intervened: It would be displeasing to the Lord; although God forgives and forgets, he doesn't remove the consequences of sin, which are frequently long term and could affect others; although his wife was far away, it could harm his relationship with her; his personal integrity would be spoiled and his testimony to the guerrillas ruined, especially with the young men in camp he called "my sons"; to really love someone means you want the best for that person, which sometimes means self-denial.

The next day Ray awakened early as usual and looked at the calendar the guerrillas had given him. November 23: Was it Thanksgiving or the week before?

"Good morning, Ramón. Did you sleep well?" Omar greeted him.

"Very well."

"Isn't this a holiday in *los Estados Unidos?*"

"Sí, es el día de gracias" ("Yes, it is a day of thankfulness").

"You know, Elise is available if you want her. It must be hard being without a woman for so long."

In an instant Ray realized God had been guarding him against this moment. "No, I have a wife waiting for me. I want to remain faithful to her."

After breakfast, Ray opened up his red New Testament from home. He looked at his name on the inside cover and remembered the day the Bible was given to him, then opened it to 1 Thessalonians 5:16–18 and read in English, "Be joyful always; pray continually; give thanks in all circumstances, for this is God's will for you in Christ Jesus." Ray could not be wholeheartedly thankful *for* his captivity, but he knew that wasn't what God was asking. He was to be thankful *in* his circumstances—finding things to be grateful for regardless of where he was or what his outlook.

Opening up his notebook, he wrote on the top of a clean page: "Thanksgiving Day, *23 de Nov. 1995 El Monte Jueves 580 días.* I hope this will be a pleasant day. God says to me today, 'Give thanks in all circumstances' (1 Thess. 5:12–28).

"Today I give thanks for my good health, friends among my captors, that I'm still alive in spite of a lifestyle like Indiana Jones, God's Word in my own language, God's mercy, God's love . . ."

Suddenly a large morfel butterfly glided past Ray, flouncing its colors of iridescent blue.

". . . God's continual reminder of his presence through nature that surrounds me, hymns and Scripture through which I hear the voice of God, good parents who loved each other, a good and faithful wife and God-fearing sons, clothes to wear, food to eat (even if it is rice and beans), and a roof over my head (a sheet of plastic).

"Isn't God good? Thank you, God!"

9

Deadly Games

November 1995 to February 1996

> For now we see in a mirror dimly, but then face to face; now
> I know in part, but then I shall know fully just as I also have
> been fully known. But now abide faith, hope, love, these
> three; but the greatest of these is love.
>
> 1 Corinthians 13:12–13 NASB

"Hey, listen to this! SIL is leaving Lomalinda!"
Always very excitable, with one ear glued to the radio, Abel
liked to be the first to announce any significant news, and
this certainly fell into that category.

Ray walked over to his own *caleta* and listened to the
broadcast on *La Voz de los Llanos* in which Larry Rahn, the
SIL director of government relations in Bogotá, made a brief
statement regarding the evacuation of Lomalinda for security reasons. Slowly Ray's eyes misted over. He had spent
much of his adult life in Lomalinda, raised his two sons
there, and the thought of its closure tarnished his happy
memories. The facility would be vacated by January 31,
1996, Rahn said. Ray looked at his calendar—November
26—that left a mere two months. Was it possible he would
be released in time to say a fond farewell to his beloved home?

"What's this all about, Lord?" Ray whispered under his breath. He turned to the Gospel of John, where he remembered reading something about Jesus teaching his disciples concepts they did not yet comprehend. What was it Jesus said in response to their confusion? There it was in John 13:7: "You do not realize now what I am doing, but later you will understand," Ray read aloud, trying to grasp what the verse meant for him.

The announcement left many unanswered questions, but one thing was certain: The Lord always gave Ray assurance and comfort in the midst of uncertainty, through his daily quiet times and by memorization of God's Word. He thought of Moses amid the fire and smoke of God's presence on top of Mount Sinai and realized he didn't need to be on the spiritual mountaintop to sense God's presence in his own life. Slowly these thoughts crystallized into one: *Did I not tell you that if you believed [in me], you would see the glory of God? (John 11:40).* Seeing God's glory was like a continual serendipity, Ray decided, one surprise after another.

A day later, Omar approached the captive with a smile on his face. "I think you may be going home soon. SIL wants a proof of life. They are asking what gift you traditionally give to your neighbor at Christmastime."

Ray thought about the question and couldn't immediately come up with an answer. Sometimes he gave gag gifts to his friends, but this question sounded like it required a more specific answer than that. Then he remembered—both he and Ray Jr. love olives but rarely bought them because of the exorbitant price. Beginning a number of years ago, they began purchasing a jar of olives for each other as a Christmas gift. That must be it!

"Olives," Ray said to the commandant in high spirits, then explained the story.

"Well, we have a gift for you." Omar handed Ray a sack. The hostage reached in and pulled out two pairs of pants and two shirts, brand-new, with the price tags still attached. All together, the clothes cost ninety dollars.

"Thank you," Ray said, perplexed. He desperately needed clothes, as his were threadbare from all the wear and tear and hand washing, but why had they bought him new clothes now? Did they want him to go home well dressed, or did it mean he would be spending more time with them?

With each passing day the hostage hoped the commandant would tell him to pack up, that he was being released. But several days passed and nothing happened. On the last day of November, some replacements came and Ray's heart sank—his release wasn't meant to be. Not yet. To his surprise, Linda began crying at the sight of the substitutes and refused to eat at the next meal. Was she feeling sorry for the captive?

"What's wrong with Linda?" Ray asked Abel after dinner.

"She's sad to have to be spending December here on this assignment. It's party month and she wants to be back with her boyfriend in another unit. When the replacements showed up, she knew it wasn't going to happen."

She's not the only one who's disappointed, Ray thought glumly.

On December 12, the captive was reading in his *caleta* when he heard a loud whirring noise behind him, growing closer and louder every second. Though the canopy of trees concealed what lay beyond them, it quickly became obvious that a surveillance plane was diving directly toward their camp. "Run, Ramón, run!" Omar yelled and lunged for his backpack.

"Come with me!" Linda ordered the captive as she ran past.

Ray ran out of the camp after Linda, with Monica and Elise following close behind. After running several hundred yards they stopped along the trail to catch their breath. A minute later Omar and a teenager named Martín ran up.

"Ramón, did you bring your things?" the commandant asked. Ray shook his head. "Martín, go back to camp and get Ray's things."

"And be sure to grab my Walkman radio and earphones," Ray added. Martín began to argue, but Ray interrupted him. "*Please* bring me my radio. It's my mental salvation!"

Martín's eyes grew wide, then he nodded and ran off.

Omar unpacked a two-way radio from his pack but couldn't make it work. "Do you know anything about these things?" he asked Ray.

Ray looked at the Yaesu FT-757GX2 HF radio. Having repaired several for his Colombian friends in the amateur radio club, he was all too familiar with it. Though he wasn't about to start repairing the guerrillas' communications equipment as a matter of course, he realized how crucial this particular radio was to his own welfare—without it, the commandant would not be able to radio for help if the hostage hurt himself, nor would he be aware if an order came to free the hostage. Ray nodded, scooted beside Omar, and began programming the frequencies into the radio's memory. Immediately the radio began working, and Ray moved back beside Linda.

"Did somebody fix the radio?" Martín asked when he returned with Ray's things, followed by several other guerrillas.

The group on the ground nodded their heads, pointing at Ray with their chins.

"Well, he can just stay with us; we need somebody like that!" Martín said.

Omar looked over at Ray and shook his head, waving his arms like a bird. Ray smiled in appreciation of the gesture—someday the captive would fly away—but wondered if it would ever really come to pass.

While the commandant radioed a few messages, Monica sorted out Ray's things and repacked his backpack. Soon they started off up the trail. As no one had scouted out the area beforehand, they had no idea which direction to head.

"I know of a place, a house beside a stream," Martín said.

Oh, boy, a house even with a thatched roof would be better than a caleta, Ray thought.

After walking about two hours they arrived at Martín's "house." It had split bamboo walls and only a partial thatched roof. It was tiny, needed a lot of repairs, and was not near a stream.

"You talk too much and are always filling our heads with gossip!" Omar said. "Wait here while Alberto and I look around."

As the commandant and Alberto scouted the area, the other guerrillas and Ray rested in and around the shelter, trying to stay out of the hot sun. Relaxing in the shade of the hut, Martín turned to Ray. "So, Ramón, how many troops do you command?"[1]

Ray gave the question serious consideration. He didn't want to lead the guerrillas into thinking he was some important military leader, but he did want them to be aware that God was looking out for him. He was still a long way from freedom and knew that even now, if given the order, the guerrillas would kill him.

"Ten thousand angels," Ray responded.

Martín's jaw dropped and his eyes grew wide. Looking at the guerrilla, Ray knew he had given the young man something to think about.

Shortly they were on the move again. After a couple of temporary locations, on December 22 they returned to a previous campsite near a ranch whose owner was known to host festive parties. Throughout that week many of the guerrillas partied away from camp, leaving only a few to guard the hostage. One evening Ray and a handful of the guerrillas sat around three candles playing Uno while the others were away. Around ten o'clock Ray excused himself from the game, entered his *caleta,* and tucked the mosquito netting in, which he did every night to keep out the rats, snakes, and larger insects. As he curled up on his palm leaf mattress, a hushed whisper startled him from one corner of his shelter.

"Ramón, come with me, quietly!" It was Monica, Omar's girlfriend.

"Who's requesting this?" Ray said, afraid to leave camp without the commandant's permission.

"Omar."

Ray quietly lifted up the mosquito net and crept into the darkness behind Monica. After several paces they met Omar, who took the captive's hand and led him and the young woman along the outside perimeter of the camp. They stole to the far side of camp, where a trail led away to the river, and hid behind a fallen tree.

After a few minutes, Alberto walked over to check on Ray, supposing he was in his *caleta.* "Hey, Ramón isn't here!" he yelled. Instantly, all of the guerrillas jumped out of their seats around the picnic table and began searching the camp in a panic. "When I find him, I'll kill him!" Alberto snarled, running by just a few feet away from the captive.

Ray's heart froze and his knees melted at the guerrilla's words. Everything within him said run, but he knew to do so would mean certain death. Just then the commandant pulled the hostage behind the food supply, and he and Monica strutted into camp. "What's going on here!" he boomed.

"We can't find Ramón," Alberto said very nervously.

"You mean you let him slip away, just like that? Ramón, come on out here!" the commandant cried.

Ray stood up from his hiding spot. Immediately Linda went over and, grabbing his arm, led him back to his *caleta.* "Don't ever do that again!" she scolded.

"It wasn't my idea," Ray explained, his knees still weak from Omar's little "game."

"Well, don't go with them next time!"

Of course, Ray had to do whatever the commandant ordered; the best he could hope for was that he wouldn't be asked to be part of such a scheme in the future.

Christmas came and went without occasion. One evening before New Year's Eve, Ray noticed his guard, Martín with an unopened book in his lap and a forlorn look on his face. Ray struck up a conversation with him.

"So, how long has it been since you've seen your family?"

"A long time. Over a year, I guess," Martín responded.

"I bet you miss them."

"*Sí*, I wish I could at least talk to them. Sometimes I think about leaving and going to a relative's, but don't tell anybody I said that!"

"Oh, no," Ray said, knowing the guerrillas' trust in him was paramount to his survival. "What happens to a guerrilla if he deserts?" he asked.

"Sometimes they're punished, but it depends on the reason why. I knew of one man who deserted and his comrades found him and brought him in for questioning. He said he was bored, so they let him go."[2]

"What's that you're reading?" the captive asked.

Martín held up the book for Ray to see.[3] "It's about the M-19's takeover of the Dominican Embassy in 1980. Pretty funny, all those unsuspecting diplomats toasting their Doble XX beer to the Day of Dominican Independence with armed guerrillas crouched at their door!"

Ray reclined again in his *caleta*. Listening to the guerrilla's propaganda disturbed him. To clear his head, he opened his Bible and picked up where he'd left off that morning in the Book of Philippians. As he read, two verses leapt from the page as if in response to his fears: Philippians 1:27–28. "Whatever happens, conduct yourselves in a manner worthy of the gospel of Christ. Then, whether I come and see you or only hear about you in my absence, I will know that you stand firm in one spirit, contending as one man for the faith of the gospel without being frightened in any way by those who oppose you." Closing the book, he praised God again for strengthening and comforting him in his time of need.

January 1996 arrived. With another dry season in full swing, the stream they were camped beside dwindled, and though the guerrillas boiled the drinking water, it was beginning to look like strong tea. Time to pack up and move. After walking for several hours, the guerrillas set up camp beside a large, fast-moving river loaded with fish—so many that all they had to do was dip their nets into the water and they were sure to draw one out. The amount of fish kept the mosquito population down, making it a nice location.

One morning Omar invited Ray to go downriver in a canoe with him and Monica to catch some *yamoo*.[4] Delighted for the opportunity to get out of camp and into the open, Ray accepted. Early the next morning he and the two pistol-carrying guerrillas headed down to the riverbank, where a large canoe awaited them on a row of logs. They pulled the canoe over the logs and into the river, then pushed off. All day long they worked the weighted nets, throwing them out over the water in front of the canoe then drawing them in from behind. Dusk had settled on the river before they returned to camp, where the commandant hollered at the others to come down and clean the fish. For several weeks they ate fish three times a day.

The rest of January passed without incident, and the days were long and lazy. On January 31, Ray was lying on a hammock in a small clearing. Looking straight up, he could see the clouds riding a breeze across the blue sky, as if on an invisible conveyor belt. He closed his eyes and imagined himself swinging in a hammock by his house in Lomalinda, surrounded by his family—what an emotionally refreshing interlude! As his daydream progressed, he sensed someone watching him. Startled, he opened his eyes to see the commandant several feet away.

"Hello, Omar," the hostage sighed.

"Do you remember when we took you? How long it's been?"

"It's hard to forget."

"Where do you want to be released?"

Ray contemplated the question, trying to recall how many times he'd heard it before. He could not afford to allow himself to get excited. "The International Red Cross would be a good place."

"I'll see what I can do," the commandant said.

Ray wondered why the guerrillas kept bringing up his liberation when, each time they moved, they seemed to migrate further away from civilization. In their own way, they were trying to be kind to the captive by giving him hope, he supposed, even if it was false hope. Or perhaps negotiations really were progressing toward his freedom. There was no way of knowing.

That night as he was preparing for bed, Ray felt an insatiable urge to turn his radio on and listen. He withdrew it from his backpack and hooked up the antenna, then scanned the dial until he came across The Voice of America. At that moment the host was interviewing Tanya Rich, wife of Mark Rich, one of the three men from New Tribes Mission still believed to be held by guerrillas somewhere in northern Colombia. Ray had been praying for Mark and his two associates—who were taken hostage over a year before his own abduction—daily while in Lomalinda and continued to do so throughout his own captivity. What an encouragement to know these men had not been forgotten by the outside world, and most likely, neither had he. After the interview he put the radio back in his pack and said his nightly prayers, including a blessing on Mark Rich, Dave Mankins, and Rick Tenenoff.

February progressed much as January had. With no sign of the military for several weeks, Ray had all but forgotten the frenzied retreats from army helicopters and surveillance planes of recent months. Then, near the end of the month, he was squatting beside the river washing dishes when he heard a helicopter coming. Seeing the advancing chopper, Abel, his guard, shouted, "Come on, follow me!" Ray bolted up the bank, sweating profusely by the time he reached the guerrilla standing nearly ninety feet away. Both men ran through the camp and grabbed their backpacks, then headed toward the jungle that lined the river. Looking up, they could see the helicopter approaching at a low altitude. Just as it passed directly overhead, they dove into the underbrush for cover.

For several minutes Ray lay on the ground, catching his breath and listening for the chopper to return. *Good, they know where I am. . . . Keep up the psychological pressure!* he thought.

Just then Abel came creeping up on all fours through the vegetation. "Do you think they saw us?"

"I hope so," Ray answered.

"What do you mean? If they see us, they'll shoot us!" the guerrilla cried.

"No, they won't shoot if they think I'm here. So it's better for you if they know where I am."

Abel gave Ray a perplexed look and shook his head. A day later Omar received a radio transmission to move on. This camp had been the best one yet, and Ray hated to leave it. Tearing down his *caleta* and packing his things, he realized it was not just that he didn't want to leave this location but that he had hoped he would never have to go through this process again—he hoped he would be liberated. As the guerrillas packed up the supplies, Pablo, who was second in command, hollered for everyone to line up.

"Not you, Ramón," he said to the captive as the others fell into place before him. The guerrillas moaned; they knew they were in for it.

"Elise, I've heard your vulgar language lately—keep that kind of talk to yourself. You help dig garbage holes in the new campsite.

" Martín Linda told me you struck her yesterday. I want twenty pieces of firewood, each five meters long, by the fire pit tonight.

"Felipe, you burned the rice two days in a row. Cook again for the next two days, and this time don't burn anything!

"Abel, for not following orders, you carry the supplies into our new camp."

As Pablo walked away, the reprimanded guerrillas groaned again while the others laughed. Finishing their preparations before the others, Ray and Abel crossed the river in a dugout canoe and waited on the other side for the rest of the guerrillas. Finally, the others loaded a large canoe with their food and equipment. Three guerrillas stepped in and positioned themselves inside the boat: Martín in the rear with a paddle, Linda in the middle, and Pablo in the bow facing Linda. Martín was an expert with the paddle and began propelling the boat with great force across the swift current. As they approached the opposite side at full speed, the bow struck a sandbar, throwing Pablo off balance. The boat tipped over, and everyone landed in the water. Linda, whose backpack and M1 carbine were on her back, went in head first, pulling her supplies and weapon in with her. As she gained her footing, she came out of the water hopping mad.

" Martín what do you think you're doing!" she yelled, pulling her M1 carbine out of the water with a shake. But seeing the others and Ray bent over in laughter, she began to chuckle too.

Taking in the scene before him of the guerrillas laughing like a bunch of kids, Ray realized these teens and young men and women were not unlike the gangs in the larger cities of his native United States. Many of them having come from single-parent homes or off the streets, abused, neglected, or simply misguided, they were all looking for a sense of family, order, and purpose in life. They had simply found it in the wrong cause. This did not excuse them from their sometimes terrorist behavior, but it helped Ray understand how ones so young could get involved in such an organization, and it filled his heart with compassion for them.

Garbled Messages

December 1995

Negotiations for Ray's release continued in steady progression from June until December 1995.[5] Just weeks before Christmas, hoping that Ray might be released before the holiday, the crisis committee requested another "proof of life" from the guerrillas. While Ray was held hostage, the committee used a variety of methods for establishing Ray's well-being, but their primary mode was to pose a question that only Ray could answer. Invariably, when the answer to the question came, everyone heaved a tremendous sigh of relief.

This time the committee submitted the question—verbally via a messenger—"What do you [Ray] typically give Brian [Gray] on his birthday?" Brian's birthday was a few days after Christmas, and usually Ray bought him a wacky hat or T-shirt. (One year, Ray gave Brian a cloth hat with a parrot beak protruding out one side. Sometimes Brian would take his handkerchief and blow the bird's nose.)

Several days passed. Finally the contact returned with the answer—olives! *Olives?!* This was a completely unexpected and extremely baffling response. Were the guerrillas taking a shot in the dark, and if so, why? Was Ray "unavailable" for consultation? Or were they dealing with the wrong people completely?[6]

Immediately, Mark called Brian and asked if Ray had ever given him olives for his birthday. No, Brian couldn't recall ever receiving such a gift. As a last resort, Mark reluctantly called Doris and relayed to her the question and the response they had received from the guerrillas. Could she sort out this puzzle? he wondered.

After some head scratching, Doris exclaimed, "Oh! Both Ray and Ray Jr. love olives, but [in Colombia] they were expensive and hard to find. So they've had a running tradition of giving each other olives for Christmas; it's the only time they ever eat them."

The connection seemed too coincidental to be chance, but the crisis team needed to know for certain. Mark checked with the messenger again, this time to find out what question had actually been asked of Ray. He replied that there had been some confusion about Brian's name, and his birthday being so close to Christmas only added to the problem. It seemed the answer fit after all, and the committee was satisfied.

All the positive signs notwithstanding, Christmas came and went with no more word from the captors. For whatever reason, Ray would not be released that year.

Difficult Times

January to March 1996

Due to Ray's kidnapping and amid threats that more could follow, SIL decided that the risks to its members living in Lomalinda were such that the time had come to close down the center. In January 1996, a tearful group of SIL personnel loaded up trucks and airplanes with all their belongings for the move to Bogotá. When the last group finally departed, only an empty shell remained of the one-and-a-half-square-mile community that had at one time buzzed with activity.

Also in early 1996, a new problem had arisen for the crisis committee: Two entities, both claiming to be speaking for Ray's captors, demanded their attention. One of these was the group Chaddy was in communication with. What a dilemma! If they chose to negotiate with one entity over the other and made the wrong choice, they risked losing Ray. Thus they tried to keep both lines of communication open.

Meanwhile, as the problem of contradictory contacts intensified and with Ray's dilemma stirring up fresh memories of their own hostage and negotiation experience, the Stendal family felt compelled to independently pursue their own dialogue with Chaddy's guerrilla contacts, which they did over a period of several weeks.

In March, with the two-year anniversary of Ray's kidnapping fast approaching, the crisis team decided to target members and friends of SIL with a prayer letter on Ray's behalf. They also prepared another leaflet to be dropped from the air over the area where Ray was believed to be held. This flyer included pictures of Doris, Ray's mother, Clarice, and Ray with Benny, a Colombian boy he'd helped with a medical problem. Perhaps people who knew Ray and had contact with the guerrillas holding him would have some influence over the captors, or maybe the guerrillas themselves would stumble onto the brochure and be moved toward compassion for their hostage and his family.

Amid the crisis team's activity of preparing the prayer letter and leaflet, the Risings' Colombian resident visas were due to expire. If they ever wanted to return to work in Colombia, it was vital to get these renewed. On March 1, Doris and Rollin flew from Charlotte to Bogotá, where they filled out the visa paperwork, caught up with old friends, and sorted through a pile of belongings from their home in Lomalinda. They'd left in such a hurry two years previous, there had been no time to go through the furniture, bedding, kitchenware, radio equipment, and so on to determine what to sell and what to ship home. Now, with Lomalinda's closure, everything sat in cartons and boxes in Bogotá.

At the end of one week of visiting, the crisis committee decided now might be a good time for Doris to make a public relations trip into Puerto Lleras. At this crucial hour, the most important thing to do was keep Ray's name alive in the hearts and minds of the Colombians who could make a difference for their friend. They asked Doris if she felt up to a visit, knowing it might reopen painful memories. She agreed.

At 6:30 A.M. on Monday, March 11, she and Rollin, along with Brian Gray and his wife, Helen, boarded a Helio Courier airplane at a small airport in Bogotá and flew through the smog and haze of the mountain plateau to Villavicencio, where they picked up a local reporter and photographer from the *Llanos 7 Días* newspaper. From there they flew to the Lomalinda airstrip, where the mayor of Puerto Lleras and a few other residents greeted them. It was the same time of year as when Ray was abducted, and the center looked the same as Doris remembered— green rolling hills turning golden from lack of rain, budding citrus trees and blooming orchids, as well as a host of other fabulous flowers in full blossom. The lake glistened in the sun, and an array of wildlife hooted and howled from the nearby jungle. Having been deserted only weeks before, the buildings had not yet begun to deteriorate; if she closed her eyes, Doris could imagine dozens of people bustling along the dirt roads and into the stores and homes. As it was, the center was lifeless and silent. One of the Colombians offered Rollin a chance to drive around the center on his motorcycle. Rollin readily agreed—he sorely missed the many afternoon and evening bike rides he used to take with his friends. Then they all headed into town.

At a sidewalk cafe, the group of Americans and their Colombian friends sat around vinyl-covered tables and talked over lunch. Lomalinda would soon be taken over by the military, the mayor said. This saddened Doris and Rollin, dashing any remnant of hope that SIL might be able to return to the translation center in the future. *God knows best,* Doris thought with a sigh. A beggar approached the table from the park across the street and asked for some money for food. Each of the *gringos* pulled a small amount of change out and gave it to the man. It wasn't much, but in this destitute region, every little bit helped.

After lunch they strolled up and down the streets of town. Dozens of men and women, recognizing the Americans, greeted them and asked about Ramón. Then the group drove to the local grade school, where early in Ray's captivity over sixty children wrote letters to Ray's captors pleading for their friend's release. Each child had had some personal experience with Ray, and now it was obvious from the flood of welcoming hugs and questions that they had not forgotten about him. Whereas Doris had always been aware of Ray's love for these people, for the first time she felt the fruit of that love. Going from classroom to classroom, with

183

the photographer's shutter clicking away, Doris thanked the children for remembering Ramón and told them she was sure even now he included them in his daily prayers. Finally, with the sun gliding down the sky toward the horizon, they boarded the airplane again and headed back to Villavicencio to drop off the reporter and photographer and refuel. With rain clouds threatening and a stormy wind commencing, they made it back over the mountains and landed just before the approaching storm let loose its fury.

On March 14, not knowing when they would meet again, Doris and Rollin reluctantly said good-bye to their friends and left for the international airport, where the strenuous task of visa, customs, baggage, and security clearance checks kept them busy for two hours. Then they boarded the northbound plane and prepared for the long ride home. As she settled into her seat and fastened her lap belt, a prayer crossed Doris's lips: *God, somehow, please use this trip to help free my husband.*

By late March the flyers to be distributed over the *llanos* were ready. On March 30, a pilot took off from Villavicencio carrying Allen Gaynor (who by that time had replaced Brian Gray as director of SIL's work in Colombia) and David Kirshman, an SIL member who recorded the event on video. With a video camera rolling, Allen leaned out the open door of the plane and tossed the brochures into the breeze. Having no idea what effect this campaign would have, the crisis team was pleased when they learned from a Colombian friend a few days later that his brother, living in the region of the drop, found several of the flyers in his yard.

> Don't forget Ramón!
> Ramón Rising was kidnapped
> the 31st of March, 1994.
> Two years in captivity!
> Why is this man still kidnapped?

What sort of person is Ramón?
- He loves and helps the neediest
- He has put most of his life into serving others

184

In [the state of] Meta:
- He administered the benevolent fund for those who needed such help
- He helped with community projects (housing, health, education, potable water, etc.)
- He coordinated medical treatment, among them surgery for Benny, burned in an accident
- He loves children deeply and the proof of this has been the number of letters written by [these children] asking for his release

Yes! You can help!
- By not forgetting Ramón
- By praying for Ramón
- By reminding people that Ramón deserves to be released

10

The Long Haul

March to May 1996

> Blessed is the man whose strength is in You,
> Whose heart is set on pilgrimage.
>
> Psalm 84:5 NKJV

The guerrillas' new campsite was again located near a river, next to a large alcove with a sandy beach that they used for bathing and swimming. On March 30, Ray and Martín were alone in the swimming hole when the hostage asked the guerrilla if he was still thinking about deserting.

"Yes, but we're too far away from civilization to do anything about it." Martín looked around to make sure no one was approaching, then continued. "Your organization dropped some brochures today from an airplane, including a couple of pictures. It contained information about your work in the State of Meta, and it appealed for your liberation. But don't tell anyone I told you about it."

Returning to camp from the swimming hole, Ray began to wonder how he could get ahold of these pictures. Entering the camp, he headed for Abel's *caleta*. Abel was acting commandant while Omar was away for a few days, and he knew the guerrilla had received orders to treat the captive well.

"Abel," Ray moaned, playing on the man's sympathies, "it's been a long time—two years—since I've heard from my family. I don't know where they are or what they're doing. My mother is ninety years old, but I don't even know if she's still alive!"

"Oh! Your organization just dropped some brochures today with some pictures of your family—" Abel stopped short, realizing he might be speaking out of line.

"Well, now, if these were pictures of your family, you would want to see them, wouldn't you?"

"We'll see what we can do," Abel said. Immediately the guerrilla conducted a brief meeting with the others, out of earshot of Ray, then returned to the captive's *caleta*.

"You may have the pictures, Ramón, but not the text," he said, holding out three pictures he had just cut from the brochure. They were of his mother, Clarice, his wife, Doris, and a picture of himself with Benny, a Colombian boy he'd helped with a medical problem a number of years earlier. The hostage tucked the pictures inside the front cover of his New Testament and looked at them often.

On the morning of April 4, Good Friday, Martín told Ray that replacements were on the way. *Oh, no,* Ray sighed. More replacements meant more time. After breakfast the hostage opened his Bible to Matthew 27 and read how Pilate secured Jesus' tomb with armed soldiers, but when the angels came, they became like dead men. *You see, Ray, it doesn't make any difference how many guerrillas there are— I am the Lord of all,* the Lord said to Ray in that still, small voice. Just then the captive looked up and saw five heavily armed guerrillas stride into camp, including Maria and Adam, and José as the new commandant. All three had left the camp a few months before, and Ray thought he'd never see them again. Yet here they were, looking like they were ready for action with their big ammo clips, grenades, pistols, and AK-47s. Ray wondered at their extra burden of weaponry. Were they prepared to protect him in case of trouble, or kill him if the military came? He thought of the two New Tribes men who were killed the year before and wondered who fired the first bullet.

As the new guerrillas began settling in, four others prepared to leave, one of them being Elise. After saying their farewells, Ray held the guerrillas' hands and prayed for them. In the presence of the replacements, Elise put her arm around Ray's neck and said, "This man has been like a father to us."

April 12 dawned with a threatening sky and a cold breeze blowing. Ray felt like huddling in his *caleta* all day, but after breakfast, José announced he had received a radio message to move the hostage further north. They needed to pack up. Late in the afternoon, after tearing the camp apart, they trekked along a trail beside the riverbank. Marching along, Pablo and Monica kept the hostage busy with endless chatter.

"So, Ramón, what's it like in *los Estados Unidos?*" Pablo asked.

"Oh, it's a big country with lots of different types of scenery. Here everything is lush and green; there you can find snow-covered mountains and vast deserts and long stretches of beach on both sides of the continent."

"Will you take us there someday?"

"Why not? Of course, you'll have to leave your weapons behind!"

The guerrillas laughed.

Coming to a large canoe, José let the others cross over first, then whispered in Ray's ear, "They're getting ready to release you, but don't tell anyone I told you." Ray hid these words in his heart and thought about them often over the

189

next several days but refused to get excited for fear of disappointment.

As the sun sank below the horizon, they stopped beside a mule trail headed north. Before they had a chance to set up all their makeshift tents, the wind whipped up and the heavens broke open in a torrent of rain. With only half the shelters erected, the guerrillas scurried every which way for cover. José, Ray, and Monica ran under one of the tarps and wrapped up together in a sheet of black plastic for warmth. For hours, the rain pounded overhead, keeping everyone awake. The time passed slowly. Suddenly they heard a loud *crrrack!* piercing through the clamor of rain. *What was that?* Finally, the rain subsided and Ray crept out from under the tarp. A tree, about fourteen inches in diameter, had broken at the base and fallen over, stopping just inches above their heads. Seeing it skimming the top of their shelter, Ray remembered God's promise from Psalm 121 that nothing bad would happen to him and said a quick prayer of thanksgiving.

The next day they walked for miles until they arrived at a storage shed beside a river, where they took off their back-breaking loads. The guerrillas opened the shed and spread out their mosquito nets and rain ponchos for bedding on the rough boards, and everyone slept for a couple hours. Around midnight, a huge dugout canoe arrived. Monica blindfolded Ray so he wouldn't see the outboard motor operator, and they all piled in. While one guerrilla shone a light on the river to see by, the driver sat in the back steering the outboard motor. In this fashion they traveled upstream for nearly an hour. Ray felt uncomfortable in the boat with a blindfold on. It reminded him of his first night in captivity.

Finally, they stopped at a farm along the river, where Monica removed the blindfold from Ray's eyes and told him to go and sit among a pile of fence posts while the guerrillas unpacked the canoe. "We're waiting for a car to come,"

Monica said, but Ray didn't believe her. He hadn't seen a car in two years, and in the darkness he saw only fields. For a long time he sat on the fence posts, swatting mosquitoes and listening to his stomach growl with hunger. Then to his surprise a car pulled up through the grass, accompanied by a motorcycle. A number of heavily armed guerrillas got out of the car, along with a woman and a pit bull, and stood by while another man introduced himself to the captive and shook his hand. Though the man did not say so, Ray surmised he was someone of importance, perhaps even the commander of the front whom Ray had written a letter to the year before. After speaking with José in low tones for a while, the man took his entourage and left, leaving the captive alone again with his traveling companions.

"All right, let's head out," José said.

"Now don't cry," Monica teased while tying the blindfold back over Ray's eyes.[1]

Putting his hands on the guerrilla's face, Ray crooned, "Monica, honey, is that you?"

Adam began to giggle. "Ramón, what a joker!" he said.

"Everyone, into the boat!" José cried out impatiently.

His anticipation building and not wanting to have his hopes dashed again, Ray tried to coerce some information from the commandant. "José, I'm scared," he said, acting frightened.

"Nothing's going to happen. Don't worry," José said.

A short boat trip later, they landed on the north shore of the river and pitched their hammocks among the leafy vegetation. After a few hours' sleep the sun came up, and they began trekking northward again. Midday, they arrived at a small lake. With his backpack on, Ray walked down to the water and dipped his fingers in, then stood up and looked around. It looked as if the pool could have been part of a main river at one time and had become separated as the water deposited silt and rocks along its shore. About twenty feet out in the water, a small alligator swam in circles. No baths in that location!

As the others set up camp, Maria and Adam went fishing. Using some old meat as bait, they threw their lines into the water. Before long they had caught a net full of piranha, which they then cut up and used as bait to catch more. As each three-pound fish closed its tooth-lined mouth around the hook, the guerrillas whipped it onto the shore where they hit the vicious-looking thing over the head with a machete. Though it took quite a few to make a meal for everyone, they fried the fish up all the same and enjoyed their unusual feast.

If the fish were fierce, the mosquitoes were even more so, and everyone had to fan themselves continually with a shirt or towel to keep from being barraged by the insects. When the sun finally went down, Ray was relieved to crawl into his *caleta,* but even then he had to fight to rid the shelter of the pesky bugs that had slipped in on his clothing. As the night deepened, the mosquitoes worsened, attacking in a fierce frenzy anyone outside the netting of their *caleta.* Even in his sleep, Ray had to be aware of where his hands and feet were lest they brush against the material and invite a handful of bites through the tiny holes in the fabric.

April 20 dawned in sweltering heat, with the mosquitoes as hungry as ever. As the guerrillas moved about the camp, swatting the pesky bugs and preparing for a new day, they suddenly heard choppers approaching from the east. Instantly, everyone stopped what he or she was doing and looked up into the hazy sky, waiting to see which direction the helicopters were heading. When they finally broke through the cloud cover, they were about a mile away on the other side of the river. Suddenly a stream of machine-gun fire aimed a few hundred yards away exploded from the sky.

"Hit the ground!" José yelled.

As the guerrillas scrambled for cover, José crept on all fours over to the captive.

"They're too close for us to run," the commandant huffed.

Ray nodded, his heart pounding.

"If we have to defend ourselves, we will." José gave Ray a grim look.

Suddenly Ray understood the gravity of the situation. "I understand," he said, then prayed silently. *Oh, Lord, is this how it ended for Steve Welsh and Tim Van Dyke? Is this how it will end for me?* He repeated Psalm 146:7, "The LORD sets prisoners free," and reminded himself of God's promise of liberation. Shortly the choppers veered off to the north and withdrew, leaving behind a frightened bunch of guerrillas and one very anxious captive.

Within a couple of days, they picked up and moved to another lake with fewer bugs. Ray set up his hammock among the trees and then opened his daily devotions by reading Luke 10:19: "I have given you authority to trample on snakes and scorpions, and to overcome all the power of the enemy; nothing will harm you." *Oh, no,* Ray thought. *What next?*

That night Ray awoke several times rolling over in the uncomfortable hammock, which he used when there was no *caleta* to sleep in. Finally, he decided to get up and use the latrine. He extended his legs over the side of the hammock and eased himself down onto his rain poncho, which covered the ground like a rug for his belongings. He began to pull his rubber boots over his toes, then thought better of it, remembering the poisonous spider he'd found in his shoe during the first month of captivity. Turning his flashlight on the boot, he saw a scorpion, about two inches long, scamper away from the beam of light. He reached out and crushed it with the butt of his flashlight, then shone the light into his boots. Nothing.

The following morning he rechecked his boots, this time inspecting his cap as well. There, in the bowl of the hat, lay another scorpion! "I don't think this spot is much better than the last," Ray said to José, holding his cap out for the commandant to see. Instantly, José dumped the arachnid out and crushed it against a tree as it attempted to crawl away.

Regardless of the scorpion sightings, José ordered camp to be set up. Soon it began to rain. It poured for days, and all the guerrillas could do was sit in their *caletas* and watch the lake rise. "Don't worry, it won't reach us," Adam said, but before long the water crept up and over its banks and began spilling into every hollow in the ground, including the little valley their camp was situated in. Soon their entire campsite was covered with a foot or more of water. For several days everyone did their best to stay dry, fixing meals and doing other tasks while the water flowed through the camp. *At least it's handy for one thing,* Ray thought, preparing for bed one night. *I don't have to leave my bed to brush my teeth!*

Lying in his *caleta*, Ray remembered the alligator he had seen in the previous lake and wondered if this lake contained alligators too. Would they swim through camp while everyone was sleeping? After a few minutes he heard Adam—who was an expert hunter—grunting out the same noise alligators make. *Glunt, glunt, glunt.* Trying to fool the guerrilla, Ray answered the call. *Glunt, glunt, glunt. Glunt, glunt, glunt* came the response, a little faster. Ray answered again, *glunt, glunt, glunt,* even quicker than before. Back and forth the guerrilla and captive went until all the guerrillas heard was a string of alligator noises. Finally, the camp burst into a fit of giggles before José ordered everyone to sleep.

In the morning Pablo walked into camp pulling a dugout canoe behind him. The guerrillas tore down the camp and loaded up the canoe, then everyone sloshed to a nearby river where another canoe awaited them. Cresting the top of the riverbank, Monica placed a blindfold over Ray's eyes. "The motor operator is apprehensive about you seeing him," she said. They traveled upriver about an hour, then got out and walked through chest-high water to higher ground.

Their next campsite was situated on what seemed like an island surrounded by water when in fact it was a small tree-crowned hill, which they shared with another guerrilla unit about one hundred yards away. Aside from the guerrillas, Ray also shared this hilltop camp with snakes, which had crept uphill to avoid the rising water. During the next several weeks, the guerrillas killed six poisonous snakes, including one coral snake that slithered in and out of the water and posed a serious threat.

Though the two units were a mere stone's throw from each other, neither camp was permitted to visit the other. But one of the guerrillas from the other unit—Lizzy, who by her own admission was very rebellious—slipped over on occasion to talk to Ray when her commandant was out. More educated than the others, she enjoyed talking to someone on her own level. Once she brought over a watch for the captive to fix. While she waited for the repair, a guerrilla named Rodrigo saw her and came over.

"Do you like Lizzy? We'll give her to you!" he said in jest.

Lizzy looked worried. "Please don't tell my commandant I'm coming over here."

Concerned that Lizzy might be discovered and reprimanded, the next time Ray saw the commandant of the other unit he approached him. "Why don't you let the guys and girls come over and visit? It would do my heart good," he said. For the next several weeks, as they waited for the floodwater to abate, the guerrillas from the other unit wandered in and out of Ray's camp freely, visiting with the captive and watching television with him.

One night toward the end of May, in preparation for bed, Ray ducked out from under the mosquito netting of his *caleta* and walked down the trail deeper into the woods toward the latrine. Immediately, Pablo rose from the guard chair and followed close behind him. Ray stopped and faced the guerrilla, who shined his flashlight into the hostage's face. Ray held up his hand to shield his eyes from the bright beam.

"I'm just going to use the latrine," he said to the guard.

"Well, I'm coming with you," Pablo answered.

Ray turned around and walked a few paces further, then faced the guerrilla again, his eyes flashing. "Pablo, you're bothering me! Do you think you could give me some privacy for once?"

Pablo looked dumbfounded and pointed his flashlight toward the ground.

The next morning Ray awoke and stretched. He looked at Pablo sitting in the guard chair. After slipping on his boots he approached the guerrilla. "I'm sorry I got angry with you last night," he said.

"Why did you get so mad?" the guerrilla asked.

"I've been a captive a long time, and everything is getting to me. I can tell I'm not normal."

Pablo nodded, and Ray walked back to his *caleta* to begin his morning devotions.

Later that day the guerrillas started hammering sticks into the ground around Ray's *caleta*. *Oh no, they're building a jail!* Ray thought. "What are you doing that for?" he asked Pablo timidly.

"It's a house. Don't you want it?" Pablo responded.

"We've been companions for two years, sharing the same conditions. Now you're building a house just for me? It doesn't seem right."

"Well, we want you to have it," Pablo said. About twenty-five-feet square, the house had a tar paper roof and sides that came up three feet from the ground. It was covered with a huge mosquito net. Inside, José set up a fifty-five-gallon drum, on top of which he placed a small black and white television. Each night the guerrillas came over and, with machine guns lying across their laps, watched programs like *El Renegado* ("The Renegade"), the news, and a Saturday night comedy program called *Sábados Felices* ("Happy Saturdays").

On May 27, José entered Ray's tar paper house with a letter in his hand. With a smile on his face he handed it to the hostage. Ray excitedly opened the letter—the first he'd received since his captivity began—and immediately recognized his friend Russell Stendal's signature. "The guerrillas have demonstrated a willingness to free you," the letter said. "The details are being worked out. We hope to have you out in twenty days."

Ray read the last line of the letter several times over before handing it back to José. He shut the television off, then lay back down on his bed and tried to imagine what the letter could mean. Since he was confident that his wife, family, and friends had all written letters in the past, the fact that this one had actually been delivered was significant. Still, anything could happen, and the letter might have been relayed to simply keep him going for another indeterminate amount of time. As conflicting thoughts volleyed through his mind, Romans 8:24–25 came to the forefront: "But hope that is seen is no hope at all. Who hopes for what he already has? But if we hope for what we do not yet have, we wait for it patiently."

Suddenly Ray knew the Lord had brought these verses to his mind to bring him unwavering hope that what God had promised, he would also accomplish. Ray opened his journal and wrote down from memory the contents of the letter. Staring at the words he'd just written, he realized that with every promise in Scripture, there is a command. God had promised him liberation; in return he required perseverance. Once more the captive set his mind to persevere and to keep his eyes on God through the long haul.

Final Proof

May to June 1996

In late May the negotiation situation hit a critical level. If Ray was ever going to be released, now was the time, yet the crisis team was still uncertain about which entity to negotiate with for his release.

As final proof, Chaddy decided to ask the guerrillas for a video of the hostage. With a video camera under his arm, he left for another one of many meetings with the guerrillas, also carrying with him a letter written by Russell to Ray telling him not to worry—he would be released soon.

Several days passed. Finally Chaddy called Mark Litz. He had the video! They set June 4 as the date for Mark and Berni Neal to fly into San Martín and pick it up. Those emotionally charged days of waiting filled everyone with anticipation. How would Ray look? Would he be thin and worn? Would he wear a smile or show signs of depression? Would his normally cheerful disposition be replaced by stoicism?

On June 3, Mark called Chaddy to confirm the meeting for the following day. To Mark's disappointment, Chaddy apologized: He was swamped. Could they put the meeting off one day? Mark reluctantly called Doris and told her she would have to wait one more day to hear how her husband was. Her response surprised and uplifted him: "Well, I'm sure the Lord has a reason for the delay."

The next day—the day originally appointed for the flight into San Martín—Dean Albany, the pilot who had flown over the *llanos* a couple months before distributing brochures and who was the pilot assigned to fly Mark and Berni into San Martín—collapsed at a restaurant during lunch. Later the doctors confirmed his condition. He had suffered a stroke. *What would have happened had they been flying that day?* Mark couldn't help but wonder. *Doris had been right. Thank God for the delay.*

The morning of June 5, Mark and Berni took a bus into San Martín, where they met Chaddy at the Stendals' home. Chaddy inserted the video into the VCR. There on the screen was a much thinner Ray, squatting on the ground and wearing a floral shirt that the guerrillas had given him. His head of hair—once brown—shone a silver gray in the muted light. As he talked to his audience, shifting his weight from one leg to the other, he looked sometimes into the camera and sometimes away at the surrounding guerrillas.

"Today's date is May 28, 1996, and this is a message to my wife, Doris, and the rest of my family and friends. I'm doing fine and look forward to the day I can be with you all again. I would appreciate whatever help you can give me to expedite my release."

He had been speaking about five minutes when the guerrillas gave him an empty tomato box to sit on, then told him to sing *"Solamente en Cristo"* ("Only in Christ"). The captive obliged:

Solamente en Cristo, solamente en El,
La salvación se encuentra en El,
No hay otro nombre entre los hombres,
Solamente en El.

Only in Christ, only in him,
Salvation is found only in him,
There is no other name found among men (for salvation),
Only in him.

199

Off camera, one of the guerrillas said, "Sing the other chorus too," referring to a song he had composed for the captive.[2]

Ray smiled. "By popular demand, I will sing another chorus written by someone here":

Oremos por Cristo, vamos a orar,
Bucamos el camino a la vida eterna, vamos a llegar.
En el camino al cielo encontramos Cristo en el paraíso
    nos esperará,
Somos sus hijos somos hermanos,
allí en el cielo vamos a llegar.

We are praying because of Christ, let us pray,
We are looking for the road to eternal life, and we are
    going to arrive.
In the road to heaven we found Christ waiting in paradise
    for us,
We are your sons, we are brothers,
We have set our sights on heaven, because that's where
    we are going.

The screen went blank, and Mark and Berni heaved a sigh of relief over how well Ray looked. Both men would sleep better that night than they had in two years, having finally seen their friend and knowing he was alive and in good health.

A Deal

June 1996

With the dilemma of which entity to negotiate with for Ray's release behind them, the crisis committee spent each passing June day deliberating over divergent points of view and proposals, as a complex and often tense dialogue narrowed down to the conditions for Ray's freedom. On June 14, a final agreement was established with Ray's captors, and the wheels were set in motion through Chaddy's contact for Ray to be released within a few days.

But the efforts of SIL and the Stendals alone did not result in Ray's liberation; the combined energy of thousands of people played an important role: the dozens who dared to put flyers in their store windows; the scores of school children who wrote letters to Ray's captors, asking them to let him go free; the handful of individuals who risked their lives as go-betweens, carrying messages and letters to the guerrillas; and the multitudes of people worldwide who prayed unfailingly for a period of over two years.

And like a powerful undercurrent that breathes life into the ocean depths, the most significant influence of all was God's Holy Spirit, at work in the hearts and minds of everyone involved, including the guerrillas themselves.[3]

Release!

June 16–17, 1996

The LORD gives freedom to the prisoners.
Psalm 146:7 NKJV

June 16, 1996, Father's Day. The middle of another rainy season in Colombia.

Will I ever be free? Ray thought in a moment of despair as he lay in his guarded hut watching the gray evening sky slowly darken. Earlier that afternoon he'd been told by the guerrillas to pack up, liberation was near at hand, but no sooner had the order come than rain began pelting the camp, thwarting his release. Judging from the swollen black clouds looming on the horizon, the storm wasn't going to let up soon. As a news broadcast droned on from the little battery-powered television in the corner of the hut, he rolled over and watched a rivulet of muddy water run underneath him from the doorway to the far wall. A weather announcement drew his attention back to the television—intermittent rain for the next twenty-four hours.

Patience, Ray told himself, turning off the television. In his mind he tried to recreate the letter he'd seen just a couple weeks before—from Russell Stendal—in which his friend wrote that he'd be liberated soon, but his mind drew a blank. *Freedom will come in God's good time,* he thought with a sigh. As he turned onto his back again, two verses from Psalm 37 that had given him comfort many times over the past two years flashed through his mind. He pulled the green Spanish New Testament with selected psalms out of his backpack and looked up the verses. "Trust in the LORD and do good. . . . Delight yourself in the LORD, and he will give you the desires of your heart" (Ps. 37:3–4). He closed his eyes and tried to meditate on what God was saying to him through the Scriptures.

During the past two years, feelings of despondency had washed over him more and more frequently. Harassment from the guerrillas that his family had forgotten him; that first Christmas in captivity in 1994 and the bittersweet memory of his wife's voice; news that two captive missionaries had been killed in 1995; running from nearby grenade and machine-gun fire—these were all but highlights in a long battle against hopelessness. Now these episodes ran together in his mind back to back, like a string of beads, and his heart sank.

Lord, you promised I would be liberated. Help me to wait! he prayed urgently. Then, like a cool refreshing breeze rustling through the *llanos,* the words of an old hymn came to mind. "Be not dismayed whate'er betide, God will take care of you; beneath his wings of love abide, God will take care of you. . . . through every day, o'er all the way . . . God will take care of you." As rain battered the tar paper roof of the hut, Ray reflected on the words. No matter what happened, even now God would give him the strength to survive just as he had in the past 809 days of captivity, he reminded himself. Slowly his muscles began to relax. He uncrossed his feet and slipped the New Testament back into his pack. As the last shreds of light filtered through the tinted netting, he fell asleep.

"Ramón, get up!" Pablo said, pointing the beam of a flashlight into Ray's face.

"What time is it?" Ray asked in Spanish that had been perfected from over two years of constant use.

"Ten-thirty. The rain stopped; time to move."

Time to move. Ray had been awakened many times with those same words. Usually they brought dread—another long night of hiking through endless brush, sloshing ankle deep through boggy marshes, or lying in the bottom of a dugout canoe. But not on this occasion! He rose quickly from his bed, pulled on his rubber boots, and grabbed his backpack. Lifting the mosquito netting, he exited the hut, then turned to look at it one last time. The clouds parted and a bright moon shone briefly on the structure and surrounding landscape. Although the hut was better than a wood frame *caleta* topped with mosquito netting and a plastic sheet, he would not miss it.

"Hurry up!" Pablo called, slinging an automatic machine gun over his shoulder. Ray followed him to a makeshift table set up in the middle of camp, normally used for preparing meals. "Let me see your backpack," he said, pointing to the pack Ray held in his hand. Ray handed him the pack, and the guerrilla spilled its contents onto the tabletop. He rummaged through the few articles: a change of clothes, a toothbrush, a hairbrush, a Spanish and English New Testament, and five notebooks. "You can't take these with you," Pablo said, sliding the notebooks under his arm.

"But those are my remembrances," Ray objected. "Please let me keep them!"

Pablo laughed. "Don Ramón, with a memory like yours, you won't need them!"

Ray shrugged in compliance. He hated to leave the diaries behind, but it was useless to argue. Arguing with the guerrillas was like quarreling with a baseball umpire: They never changed their minds! Pablo filled a plastic bag with the remaining items and handed it to Ray. Just then José, Rodrigo, and Cosmo walked up. José thrust out his hand.

"I will miss you, Don Ramón. You put up with my singing!" the guerrilla said.

"I'm grateful for the chorus you composed for me," Ray replied. "Thank you for your help and encouragement."

Turning to Rodrigo, he said, "Thank you for your friendship; it has meant a lot. I'll keep praying that you will be able to return to your family." Rodrigo shook the captive's hand and nodded his farewell.

Ray faced Cosmo. "I'm glad you're letting Lizzy and Monica walk out with me. Thanks for the tar paper house, and for loaning me your TV."

Ray completed his farewells and nodded at Pablo, indicating he was ready to go. Looking at the hostage, the guerrilla said to his companions, "Ramón is very dear to lots of people, eh?" The other guerrillas nodded in agreement.

"Comrades, let's go!" Pablo called, and immediately six machine-gun-carrying guerrillas began filing out of camp. Ray followed Pablo and two of the guerrillas, as four others took up the rear. For half an hour they trudged up and down the muddy path leading to a nearby river. The air was hot and heavy with moisture following the deluge. Ray's shirt dripped with sweat and clung to his chest and back. As he tramped along, he felt something prick his left arm just above the elbow. He looked down to see a large conga ant stinging him with its poisonous venom through his shirt sleeve; he flicked the pesky insect off and rubbed his arm. *That'll hurt for a few hours.*

Approaching the river, the trail suddenly dropped off down a steep bank. Ray slid down the bank several feet before his boots sunk into the mud and stopped him. Suddenly a strong hand grabbed his arm and pulled him to his feet. Looking up into the man's face, Ray did not recognize him, but it was obvious from his demeanor that he was a commander within the guerrilla organization. Standing by his side was his wife, who looked curiously at Ray.

"Haven't they given you a gun yet?" the commander said with a laugh.

"No, I keep asking, but they won't let me have one," Ray answered wryly. He'd learned long ago the best way to survive each day was with a sense of humor, to which the guerrillas readily responded. The commander laughed.

At the bottom of the trail, Ray, the woman, and the eight captors took seats in a waiting canoe and shoved off across the narrow river. On the other side the trail continued through waist-high grass, still warm and moist from the rain and sweltering night air. As he marched through the grass, he felt a *sting . . . sting . . . sting* across his back, chest, and arms. Looking down at his shirt, now bathed in moonlight, he saw a black layer of mosquitoes. Irritated, he swiftly brushed them away with a swoop of his hands. He'd been bitten so many times over the last two years it was a wonder he hadn't developed an allergic reaction, he thought. As they waded along the grassy path, Ray kept pulling the soaked fabric away from his skin trying to avoid any more bites.

Shortly they came to a road—parallel tire tracks laden with *arrecife*[1]—where an open vehicle sat idling in the tall grass. The commander sat beside the driver as Ray, the commander's wife, and a couple of the guerrillas squeezed into the backseat. The others stood on the bumper and clung to the vehicle's back and sides. With everyone aboard, the car roared off through the grass, frequently slipping off the *arrecife* and into the mud, then back onto the road again.

After a few minutes, the commander's wife groaned, putting her hand up to her forehead. Ray looked at her inquisitively.

"I have a headache," she said.

"Is it a sinus headache?" Ray asked.

"No, I'm just nervous."

"You don't need to be nervous. You're with me and I'm with God so nothing bad is going to happen to us!" the captive said, remembering God's promise to him from Acts 27:24 that he and all that were with him would be granted safe passage wherever they went.

The commander's wife looked at Ray for a moment, her eyes filled with amazement.

After an hour they came to a stop at a fork in the road. "We're coming up on some towns. Blindfold him," the commander ordered.

An awkward silence filled the car. Finally, Lizzy, who was sitting in the rear jump seat, passed Ray a sweatshirt and told him to blindfold himself with it. "Thank you, Lizzy," Ray responded. "I couldn't understand what he said."

Ray slipped the sweatshirt over his head and tied the sleeves around to keep it from shifting. Soon he conjectured from the smoother ride that they were on a maintained road, and the hum of the engine indicated their speed was diminishing. Here and there he heard voices on either side of the car, then silence. Suddenly the car stopped with a jerk.

"We'll get out here and have something to eat," the commander said.

The car door opened and Ray was instructed to remove the sweatshirt from his head. He did so, and instantly the night air blew against his sweaty face. He breathed in deeply and stretched. Sitting four across in the backseat was hot enough without having his head covered.

It was now past midnight, and the sky had clouded over again, though no rain fell. He followed the others into an isolated adobe house where a woman stirred a large aluminum pot over the fire. They all helped themselves to pieces of chicken, baked potatoes, and yuca from the pot. The repast came as a welcome surprise; his last meal—lunchtime the previous day—consisted only of a tortilla, rice, and broth.

Before long the interlude ended. As before, Ray was told to wrap the sweatshirt around his head as they all piled back into the vehicle. They had not gone too far when the car rumbled to a halt. Pablo reached from behind and uncovered Ray's head, then Ray and his guards climbed out, leaving the driver, the commander, and his wife inside the car. The vehicle left and Ray followed the guerrillas along the side of the dirt trail. Knowing at last that his release was imminent, he eyed the row of guerrillas walking before him. Not one of them was over the age of twenty-five. What would become of them? he wondered.

They walked until 2:30, then stopped and sat down in the grass just off the trail and waited. After a few moments, Pablo, who liked to tease, spoke up. "Will you miss Lizzy?"

"Yes, but I will miss Pablo too."

Pablo bellowed back, *"Gracias!"* Suddenly a rooster crowed nearby. "Hey, Ramón," Pablo shouted, "there's a *pici sucio*" ("dirty pecker," because chickens peck the dirt).

"Send Curly to get it for me!" Ray responded.

"Hey, Curly, catch the chicken!" Pablo shouted. A guerrilla with stick-straight hair leapt from the ground and began searching for the chicken but returned when he heard the sound of soft rustling grass. Someone was approaching. Soon a dark-skinned man with a bent arm, Omar, and two other guerrillas Ray did not know approached.

"Ramón!" Omar said.

"Hello, Omar. So you are my leader once more?"

"Only for a short time. We need to hurry."

Knowing they would not be traveling the rest of the way with the captive, the guerrillas, except for Adam, quickly lined up to say good-bye. One by one they filed past Ray.

"Curly, you're such a cutup! Thanks for making me laugh," Ray said to the straight-haired guerrilla. Curly laughed.

"Sorry we were together for just a short time," Ray said to Felix. "It would have been nice to get to know you better. Take care of Lizzy for me."

"Lizzy," Ray said, taking the young girl's hands in his, "you were a great relief to me because you wanted to be my friend; you even took some risk to be my friend. I'll never forget that. The Bible says true beauty is of the heart. You may be somewhat rebellious, but that's what I like about you. We have to accept each other for who we are. God bless you."

"Monica, thank you for the good food you prepared and for your friendship. God bless you." Ray gave her the customary kiss on the cheek.

Next, he shook the hand of Tomas, who had spent only a short time with him. "Thank you for being a good friend to me," the captive said.

At the end of the line was Pablo. "Words cannot express my gratitude to you," Ray began. "Thank you for your friendship for, what, thirteen months? Each day, you never failed to look in on me and make sure I was doing all right. You always helped me set up camp, and your cooking was the best! Your presence greatly comforted me. God bless you, and I will pray for you." As Ray shook Pablo's hand, he slipped his Buck penknife into the guerrilla's palm. Pablo looked up in surprise but did not say anything.

"You ready?" Omar asked. Ray nodded, then followed Omar, his two companions, and Adam along a muddy path that led gently downhill toward the banks of a wide river. There, once again, was a canoe at their disposal, but entering the craft Omar discovered there were no paddles. "We'll have to pole across." Omar picked up the poles normally used only to push the canoe away from shore. As they entered the swift current, he and another guerrilla tried digging the poles into the sludgy river bottom, but soon the water was too deep and the poles would not reach. Anxiously the two men paddled as best they could with the poles. The canoe circled around in the current several times but eventually drifted close enough to the other shore so that the poles again reached the bottom. For some time the men strained against the poles until the canoe reached the other bank, where everyone disembarked and trudged quickly up the muddy slope.

At the top of the embankment, Omar stopped and surveyed their surroundings. "Looks like we drifted too far west; the trail must be that way," he said, pointing to his right. Cutting through the grass at the top of the embankment, the four guerrillas and Ray marched along, slapping mosquitoes as they went. "We need to walk quickly," Omar instructed. They picked up their pace.

In the fading moonlight, Ray scanned the gently rolling hills to his left; none of it looked familiar to him. Could they be lost? For several minutes he anxiously followed his captors until they found the trail. For what seemed like another hour, Omar led the little band north along the trail at a fast clip. Covered with mud and sweat, Ray continued to slap at the bugs as they attacked from the air and the ground. At four o'clock, they came to another road and stopped. "We'll wait here," Omar said.

The five men waited in silent darkness for an hour—the guerrillas sitting in a circle on the edge of the road, cigarettes dangling from their mouths and machine guns across their laps, while Ray stood nearby. Five o'clock rolled around, and a fine drizzle began falling. Seeing a tree up the road, the hostage started for it.

"Hey, where are you going?" Omar yelled, jumping to his feet, gun ready.

"To get out of the rain," Ray answered, pointing to the tree.

211

Omar relaxed but kept a watchful eye on Ray as he ambled up the road. From beneath the thick boughs of the tree, Ray watched the sky turn a pale pink as the rising sun illuminated the edge of the horizon, then disappeared behind a wall of gray. Shortly, Omar called him back.

"Hey, uh, Monica's been acting like she's mad at me," Omar said, sidling up to the captive. "Do you know why?"

"Probably because she feels you abandoned her," Ray said.

For several minutes they stood in silence, then the distant hum of motorcycles broke the stillness.

"Duck down in the brush," Omar said.

Ray crouched in the tall grass with his sack between his legs.

"More! I can still see you!" Omar demanded.

Ray squatted down further until his nose was barely inches off the ground. The noise of motorcycles grew closer as two bikes advanced from a distance. Omar, his two companions, and Adam took a defensive stance in the road, not completely sure who was approaching. Finally, the bikes stopped beside the guerrillas. Crouched down as he was, Ray could not see the riders.

"We're looking for Ramón Rising," one of the riders said. Ray recognized the voice of his good friend Chaddy.

"Ramón!" Omar called out.

Ray rose from the grass to see Chaddy straddling one motorcycle while a Colombian civilian sat astride another. Two more guerrillas, who were standing beside the bikes, had ridden behind Chaddy and the Colombian.

"Ray!" Chaddy yelled, nearly knocking his bike over in an attempt to reach his friend. "You look good," he said, choking back tears and holding Ray's thin shoulders at arm's length.

"I feel great," Ray responded tiredly. The two men hugged.

Turning to the two guerrillas he did not know, Ray gestured toward Chaddy with his chin. "I've known this man since he was your age," he said. The two guerrillas, holding rifles and staring innocently at him, were not much more than boys.

"Adam," Ray said, taking the middle-aged man's hand. "God bless you, and thank you for your friendship during difficult circumstances. You respected me and my Christian faith and defended me. God knows all of us very well, remember that. Tell Maria good-bye for me. Maybe someday, God willing, I will return to Colombia for a visit."

Finally, he turned to Omar. "We will be friends for life, because of what God's done between us. It's like something written in concrete. Thank you for all your help, and especially for loaning me your radio on Sundays so I could listen to Christian programs. That meant a lot to me." Omar nodded.

"Hop on," Chaddy said, patting the seat of the bike.

With the Colombian civilian as an escort, Ray and Chaddy drove up the road, leaving the guerrillas behind. Ascending a rise in the road, Ray looked over his shoulder. Omar and his companions stood in the middle of the road, guns poised, watching as he drove off. Ray contemplated them for a moment longer, speculating on God's sovereign purpose in allowing him to be taken captive 810 days previous. Suddenly a thought entered his mind, a Bible verse he'd read several times over the past two years. "[God] is patient with you, not wanting anyone to perish, but everyone to come to repentance" (2 Peter 3:9). How were the guerrillas to hear the message unless someone brought it to them? Ray sighed, sensing the pleasure of his Lord. He had planted the seed.

Omar and the others dropped out of sight as Chaddy's motorcross bike descended the crest of the rise. Ray fixed his eyes on the road ahead. Muddy, with saturated grass bent and lying across the *arrecife* tracks, it was the most beautiful road he'd ever seen.

Good News!

June 11–17, 1996

On June 11, Doris received a copy of the proof-of-life video Chaddy had procured from the guerrillas. She punched it into her VCR and played the tape several times. Though still a long way from being safe, seeing her husband and hearing the sound of his voice gave her comfort beyond words.

Over the next few days, she received almost daily calls from Mark Litz, updating her about the progress of their negotiations with the guerrillas. Then on Sunday, June 16, he called to say he had good news: The crisis committee had struck a deal with Ray's captors. "We should have him by the end of the week," he said.

"I'll believe it when I see the whites of his eyes," Doris replied. Months of getting her hopes up only to have them dashed had taught her to remain guarded and practical.

Monday morning, June 17, Doris went to the JAARS center, where she worked to keep busy while Ray was gone. At noon she drove home and ate lunch. As she was looking through the mail, the phone rang.

"Doris? This is Mark. Hey, don't leave the house. I think you'll be receiving an important phone call pretty soon!" Doris sensed the excitement in his voice; the mail she still held in her hand slipped from her fingers and scattered over the kitchen floor.

"It's over then?" she said quietly.

"Yes. Ray's in San Martín with Chaddy. He should be in our hands this afternoon."

Doris hung up the phone in a state of ecstasy—Ray was alive and free! For the next half hour she hopped around the house, flitting from sofa to chair to the front porch, then back to the sofa again, waiting for the telephone to ring. She tried to read but found herself scanning the same words over and over again. Hands trembling, she rinsed her lunch dishes and loaded them into the dishwasher. Finally, the phone rang.

"Hi, honey; it's me!"

"Oh, Ray, I can't believe I'm finally talking to you! Are you okay?"

"I'm fine. Don't worry, I'll be home soon. We'll see each other soon!"

Doris spent the rest of the afternoon on the phone, calling her family and friends and telling them the good news. All the sleepless nights, endless questions, and agonizing worries were indeed finally over. Though they still did not understand it, and perhaps never would, God had accomplished his purpose, and it was time for Ray to come home.

> Since the Lord is directing our steps, why try to understand everything that happens along the way?
>
> Proverbs 20:24 TLB

Conclusion

Illuminating the Path

> The ultimate measure of a man is not where he stands in
> moments of comfort and convenience, but where he stands
> at times of challenge and controversy.
>
> Martin Luther King Jr.

Sometimes the hardest thing about writing
nonfiction is knowing where a good story ends. That's
because oftentimes the ending is still being written in the
pages of history while the story is being told. Such is the
case with the kidnapping, captivity, and liberation of Ray
Rising; the story just keeps going on and on.

At the time of his release, many people sensed that we
hadn't seen "the end" yet. With this book only a vision in
the future, I thought surely by the time of its completion
there would be some sort of closure that would bring the
story full circle. But with each "ending" (the closure of
Lomalinda, Ray's farewell to the guerrillas, his deliverance
into the hands of friends, and so on) a new door has opened,

lighting the path to a new beginning. As a friend who loves Colombia and works diligently to better the lives of its people once told me, "We will not be satisfied that we've seen the end of this story until we see the guerrillas and the military, one by one, lay down their weapons and embrace each other in the truth of God's love." Indeed, that would be a *great* ending!

As the future unfolds, we may never discover all the ways in which God used Ray's story. Here are just a few "endings" and "beginnings" that have come about since the captive started down that muddy road to freedom.

First, what happened to the ex-captive? As the sun illuminated an overcast sky that morning of June 17, 1996, Ray and Chaddy, along with their Colombian companion, rode along a path that cut through the *llanos* and met with another road. This byway, lined with farmers' fields, is normally a quiet one, and after the previous day's downpour, no one had ventured out that morning. Their ride was slow going, as the wheels of the two dirt bikes struggled to find traction in the thick mud and frequently splattered both drivers and rider. Sometimes Chaddy had to drive off the road into the slick grass to avoid the deep, mucky holes in the road.

As they rode along, Ray filled Chaddy's ears with questions about his family and friends. Though happy to hear that his wife and sons were safe, confirmation of Lomalinda's closure saddened him. Chaddy explained that after a quick stop at a nearby farm, they would find his truck, which he had driven as far as it would go without getting stuck in the mud, and head toward San Martín.

At the farm, Chaddy's brother, Russell, waited anxiously for their arrival. Seeing the two cycles approach, he ran out of the house and flashed Ray a broad smile. The two men hugged and cried, each understanding the other's experience in captivity.[1]

218

Ray washed up and changed his clothes. He was still wearing the dark green uniform he'd been given by his captors and didn't want to be seen traveling through an auto-defense-controlled area dressed as a guerrilla.

Soon they were off again, this time with Russell riding behind the Colombian. They neared *Pueblo Seco* (Dry Town), a small outcrop of buildings alongside the otherwise secluded dirt road. The truck was up ahead, Chaddy said, just past a familiar day care center. Shortly, they began passing a few people walking along the road. Ahead, a knot of men and women stood to one side. As the riders passed on their motorcycles, the group stared at the comical sight of the two bikes, tires slipping first one way then another, carving up the thick mud like a spatula slicing through paint on a palette. Suddenly, one of the ladies, a stocky woman from Puerto Lleras, began pointing and screaming. "Don Ramón! Did you see him? That was Ramón Rising!"

Chaddy kept on driving, hoping the woman would decide she was mistaken. The crisis committee wanted Ray to leave the country as quickly as possible without being seen. But it was no use. As they traveled the few remaining hundred feet to the truck, they could hear the woman's voice trailing behind but growing nearer. The men stopped at the truck and Russell and Ray hopped off the bikes. As Chaddy and the Colombian prepared to drive the cycles back into town, the woman appeared, huffing and puffing, around the last bend in the road. With Ray clearly in her sights, she cried out again, a jumble of sound mixed with sobs of happiness. This time Ray could not ignore her. He allowed the woman to catch up with him, standing now beside the open passenger door of the white truck, where she hugged him and gave him the customary kiss on both cheeks.

"Now, you can't tell anyone you saw us," Russell warned her. "You need to keep this quiet for at least eight days. Do you understand?"

219

The woman, eyes gleaming, nodded her head. *"Sí,"* she said, but Ray doubted she would be able to contain the news for that long.[2]

After a few more tears and hugs, Russell and Ray took off in the truck and traveled the rest of the distance to the Stendals' home in San Martín, where Chad Sr. (Russell and Chaddy's father) greeted his longtime friend. There Ray took a shower—his first in over two years—and lay down on a real mattress for a rest while Chaddy made arrangements for Ray's journey to Bogotá. After his respite, Ray spoke briefly to Doris, assuring her that he was okay and would see her soon.

At 4:30 in the afternoon, an SIL pilot, Berni Neal, and Ray Jr., who had been working in Bogotá at the time, arrived in a Helio Courier airplane. As the engine of the aircraft wound down, Ray met his son on the airstrip, where they embraced and cried. Then everyone, including Chad Sr., piled into the plane and flew from San Martín to Villavicencio, where they switched to a King Air plane and flew to Bogotá. The next day the ex-hostage had a physical and visited with friends, then spoke to the entire SIL community there, many of whom had been his neighbors in Lomalinda.

The following day, Ray boarded an American Airlines flight destined ultimately for Charlotte, where his family and a few friends welcomed him. The next few days were spent at the Billy Graham conference center in Asheville, North Carolina, where Ray was debriefed and he and his family talked with a group of counselors who could guide the family through the readjustment period. Finally, Ray and Doris returned to Waxhaw, where they are currently living. Since his release, Ray, along with Doris, has traveled extensively throughout the United States, sharing his experiences, praising God for the blessings, and requesting prayers on behalf of the Colombian people.

SIL's departure from Lomalinda in January of 1996 is still a painful memory for many of its members. The green rolling hills, the grasslands of *Finca Bonaire*, the jungle-lined lake, along with the grocery store, post office, school, chapel, and brick-clad houses, all formed the community called "home" by dozens of families. Many gave birth and raised their children there; all did translation and other support work there to bring God's Word to Colombia's indigenous people. Some even died there and were laid to rest in the cemetery grounds, where little white crosses still mark their graves.

Its closure was a great loss, a defeat to the cause of Christ, some say. As if to punctuate their position, they suggest that if it hadn't been for Lomalinda—God's presence in the land—the surrounding area would have succumbed to violence much faster than it did. Others do not see the closure as a defeat, feeling it is better to be alive and continuing the work of Bible translation than for the work to be extinguished (along with the SIL workers) in a region of the country where violence seems to climb with each sunrise. Yet, both sides acquiesce on one point: All the "what ifs" and "if onlys" diminish in the light of God's sovereignty. Ultimately, the Almighty One alone is responsible for getting his will accomplished, in his own time and way.

Like a seed that must first die before it can spring forth in new life, a new dream blossomed from the demise of Lomalinda. After the center closed its doors for the last time, turning over the keys to the Colombian government (the military now occupies the property), many of the SIL workers moved their work and their lives to Bogotá and several other Colombian cities. There they found new homes and new friends, as well as a greater opportunity to interact with the evangelical Colombian church, which, in recent years, has been developing its own mission vision to evangelize indigenous groups within its vast homeland. Due at least in part to the presence of SIL in their midst, these Christian brothers and sisters are gaining invaluable knowledge and experience in building an effective cross-cultural missions foundation.

With Ray's ordeal at an end, the members of the crisis committee returned to the ministry for which they had originally come to Colombia: bringing the Word of God to that country's indigenous people. Some remained in Colombia; others went on to different places of service. All were grateful that God granted Ray his freedom and happy to have been a part of his release.

After the closure of Lomalinda, SIL sold *Finca Bonaire* to Chaddy Stendal, who grows crops and raises brahma bulls there (with the aid of a few Colombian employees) while his brother, Russell, hopes to utilize the property to host conferences for believers in the community. Because of their contacts, the Stendals are able to conduct missionary work in the area, unhindered by guerrilla intervention. Russell also works alongside Chad Sr. performing missionary work with the Kogi Indians near the North Coast region of Colombia.[3]

Approximately fifty guerrillas passed in and out of Ray's camp during his 810 days in captivity; some stayed only for a few weeks, while others stayed for months at a time. The ones mentioned by pseudonym in this book were the most memorable to Ray. Whether in groups or on an individual basis, they came to know what Ray stood for and to whom he pledged his allegiance. "I realized if I wasn't a person of integrity, I wasn't anything," Ray has said since his ordeal. "I had to be that, for my testimony to them, for my family, and for my responsibility before God."

This is not to say Ray didn't make mistakes, didn't succumb at times to frustration, impatience, or discouragement. But in the midst of the human condition, he did his best to follow hard after God, choosing the cost and blessings of the cross over the price of compromise.

> But the good man—what a different story! For the good man—the blameless, the upright, the man of peace—he has a wonderful future ahead of him. For him there is a happy ending.
>
> Psalm 37:37 TLB

Epilogue

Your kingdom come, your will be done [in Colombia] . . . as it is in heaven.

Matthew 6:10

During the first weeks of my captivity, I was greatly grieved that I had fallen into such a bad situation. Of course, all I could think of was the "what ifs"—what if I hadn't gone into town that day, what if Doris had gone with me? It was like wishing the whole experience was a bad dream and that I would wake up from it in the peace and comfort of my own home. But over and over again God reminded me that when my faith is tried, it is also purified. First Peter 1:7 says that through tribulation my faith, which is "much more precious than gold that perishes, though it is tested by fire, [will] be found to praise, honor, and glory at the revelation of Jesus Christ" (NKJV).

Over and over again throughout the days, weeks, months, and years of my captivity, I, like Paul, found comfort for my downcast heart (2 Cor. 7:6) through God's Word and daily circumstance. Knowing that my situation would help me experience God's presence in an even greater way gave me courage to believe that he was in control of everything, and not only in control, but ordering the events of my life for my own spiritual good. "'For I know the thoughts that I think toward you,' says the LORD, 'thoughts of peace and not of evil, to give you a future and a hope'" (Jer. 29:11 NKJV).

Another great lesson I learned from my captivity was that God is a caring God. First Peter 5:7 says I can cast all my cares on him, because he cares for me. To care means to encourage, or build up. Hebrews exhorts us to "encourage one another," while Romans states that "the gifts and calling of God are irrevocable." This means God expects me to care for others.

One of the first guerrillas I encountered knew people I knew, one of whom had been assassinated. As time went on, I became aware that this was an experienced guerrilla fighter, yet God provided opportunities for me to care for him, both physically and spiritually. As I repaired his Walkman, I also talked to him about his soul. At the end of the first month, he was sent back to the main unit with a disciplinary letter because of his friendship with me. Did God preserve my life by my caring for others? Did my care for the guerrillas help them in any way?

Another way God cared for me was by taking care of my family. I would like to take this opportunity to thank my fellow workers, in Colombia and the States, who prayed for me and attended to my family in my absence.

In a rapidly changing and sometimes brutal world, we need to care for and encourage each other more and more. Colombia is no exception. A beautiful country in the midst of a violent conflict, its people are kind and gracious, especially the children and young people, who are the real victims of this tragedy. Half of my captors were teenagers. Many came from broken homes or were orphans. As I think of these people today, my heart still grieves for them, as does the heart of God. They are the product of social ills in that country that only Christ can cure completely. To be a servant of Christ to these people is indeed a great privilege.

At the end of 1995, I tied a paper peace flag to my *caleta* for everyone to see. When asked about it, I said I have peace with God through Jesus Christ my Lord. Peace is a precious commodity in Colombia. Daily, I pray for peace and reconciliation in that land, knowing that ultimately they come only from God and are based on personal renewal with him. Only then can peace be extended to one another.

Ray Rising

Afterword

I cannot know what your destiny will be, but one thing I do know is that the truly happy among you will be those who have learned to serve.

Albert Schweitzer

How did Ray Rising survive his captivity? He was rooted in faith, grounded in the Word of God. Throughout his ordeal, God's Word provided him encouragement, strength, and hope.

Today there are over 440 million people who do not have access to a single verse of Scripture in their heart language. They face the difficulties of life without the hope found in the gospel. Wycliffe Bible Translators believes that every man, woman, and child should have the Scriptures translated into his or her own language. Wycliffe believes God's Word—and the intimacy it can bring with Jesus Christ—can instruct, inspire, encourage, and nurture people in all aspects of their lives.

Over six hundred years ago, John Wycliffe risked everything to translate the Bible into the heart language of his people, the English-speaking people. It was a radical idea then, and it is still a radical idea today.

Nearly sixty years ago, Wycliffe Bible Translators' founder, Cameron Townsend, took hold of John Wycliffe's vision and ran with it to the ends of the earth. Today, translators and support personnel work in over fifty countries in partnership with national translators, Bible societies, local Bible translation organizations, churches, and individuals to provide the Word of God to those who otherwise might not ever hear it in their own language. The Wycliffe team is diverse—from accountants and linguists to school teachers and mechanics, from computer engineers to communication specialists, all working together to see a dream realized. The task is overwhelming but not impossible. The work ahead of us is God-directed, and we look to his resources to provide the people, prayer, and funds needed to complete the work.

There is a place for each individual on this team, supporting our work through prayer, helping fund a portion of the work, or serving in the work. If you'd like to know more about how you can help us finish the goal of bringing the Word of God to every man, woman, and child, contact us. We'd like to share our vision with you. Call (800) WYCLIFFE or contact us through our web site at www.Wycliffe.org.

Serving the Bibleless people,
Roy Peterson
Executive Director
Wycliffe, USA

Appendix

List of Names

With the exception of Ray Rising and his family, the Stendal family, and Chester Bitterman and the five New Tribes missionaries referred to in chapters 7 and 9, all the names of individuals identified in this book have been changed. This has been done to protect them from any difficulties or harm stemming from their involvement in helping secure Ray's freedom.

Guerrillas

Arnoldo—commandant March 31–August 2, 1994
Omar—commandant August 2, 1994–January 24, 1995, and October 15, 1995–April 4, 1996
Jaime—commandant January 24–October 15, 1995
José—commandant April 4–June 17, 1996

SIL Personnel

Dean Albany—pilot
Jim Fleming—member of Lomalinda security team
Karen Fleming—Jim Fleming's wife

Allen Gaynor—took over the role of director of SIL's work in Colombia from Brian Gray in January 1995

Brian Gray—director of SIL's work in Colombia until January 1995. He remained on the crisis committee after passing on the title of director to Allen Gaynor.

Helen Gray—Brian Gray's wife

George Kavanaugh—chairman of the crisis committee in Colombia until June 1995

Katie Kavanaugh—George Kavanaugh's wife

David Kirshman—SIL member

Mark Litz—replaced George Kavanaugh as chairman of the crisis committee in Colombia in June 1995

Ed Mann—head of security for SIL in Colombia

Berni Neal—crisis committee member

Larry Rahn—director of government relations in Bogotá

Mary Smith—translator for *Radio Periódico al Minuto* radio broadcast

Notes

Introduction: Beginnings

1. Colombia comprises jungles, fertile plains, and the northernmost portion of the Andes mountain range. It is rich in coal, emeralds, and several precious metals.

2. This phrase, taken from Gabriel García Márquez's novel, *One Hundred Years of Solitude* (trans. Gregory Rabassa [New York: Harper & Row, 1970]), has been coined as representative of the attitude of Colombians amid the violence that ravages their country. Interestingly, Alvaro Fayad, former *commandante supremo* of the M-19 Revolutionary Movement, once said García's text was the only required reading for a Colombian revolutionary.

3. With the formation of the "National Front" (between the liberals and conservatives), all other opposing activities became criminal, driving any dissident politics underground.

4. Undesirables included not only opponents to the guerrillas but criminals, drug users, homosexuals, and others who might present a drain to society.

5. The *llanos* are the plains, or grasslands, interspersed about the jungle.

6. For example, as early as the mid-1970s, with political shifts in the U.S.S.R., funding for the communist-backed forces in Colombia decreased dramatically.

7. Although actual figures vary, the revenue brought into the guerrilla movement from the drug trade is measured in the multimillions of dollars. See Major Luis Alberto Villamarín Pulido, *The FARC Cartel* (Bogotá:

Ediciones El Faraón, 1996); and Jesus E. La Rotta M., *Las Finanzas de la Subversion Colombiana* (Santafé de Bogotá, 1996).

8. Ana Carrigan, *The Palace of Justice—A Colombian Tragedy* (New York: Four Walls Eight Windows, 1993), 31.

9. "Kidnapping insurance" insures an individual against the event of a kidnapping. If the insured person is kidnapped, the insurance carrier pays a prearranged, set fee.

10. The auto-defense units are made up of civilians who have banded together against the guerrillas. Their strategy is to "suck the water from the fish," meaning they want to extract the guerrillas from a given area by striking more terror into the hearts of the *campesinos* of retaliation from the auto-defenses than from the guerrillas.

11. Javier Giraldo S. J., *Colombia—The Genocidal Democracy* (Monroe, Maine: Common Courage Press, 1996).

12. Still, Colombia is the number two exporter of cut flowers in the world, second only to Holland.

13. The Summer Institute of Linguistics is the sister organization of the Wycliffe Bible Translators.

14. "Heart language" refers to a person's native tongue as opposed to the national language of the country in which he or she lives.

15. Today, working in partnership with national translators, local churches, Bible societies, and various organizations, SIL personnel work in over 50 countries in 1,053 language groups. Since 1934, over 450 New Testaments have been completed in the languages of more than 30 million people.

16. Today, of the 6,700 known language groups in existence worldwide, over 2,000 are still without a written language.

17. In 1942, Camp Wycliffe incorporated under the name Summer Institute of Linguistics (SIL) in connection with the University of Oklahoma. Today, SIL's main headquarters is in Dallas, Texas. Each year, over one hundred new translators begin a two-year training program hosted in eight countries.

18. One of the world's foremost experts in the study of tonal systems and phonology, Dr. Pike has been nominated for a Nobel Peace Prize every year since 1982 and has received many other prestigious awards over the years.

19. As a specialist in electronics, Ray's field of expertise fell under the administrative umbrella of JAARS.

20. After his release from guerrilla captivity, Ray expressed his appreciation for these three months of jungle training, which helped him survive his ordeal.

21. Especially after Colombia's experience with Germany during World War II, suspicions ran high concerning foreigners living in their lands. At this particular time, some suspected Lomalinda was the location of a clandestine uranium mining operation, while others believed it to be a front for U.S. intelligence.

22. Because of its position along the banks of the Ariari River at a major ferry crossing, Puerto Lleras is the gateway to guerrilla territory in much the same way as Dodge City, Kansas, was the portal to the western frontier during the 1800s.

Chapter 1: Kidnapped!

1. These lottery funds went to such organizations as the Colombian Red Cross.

2. *Finca Bonaire* is a farm outside of but adjacent to Lomalinda. It was used to train indigenous people, and its cattle program enabled these people as well as local farmers to improve their herds. Also, through its cattle and crops, it was a source of food and income for the translation center and a means of employment for some of the local Colombian residents.

3. This crisis committee consisted of SIL members located in both Lomalinda and Bogotá. During the course of Ray's captivity, these members interacted in person and over the telephone.

4. The crisis committee wanted to eliminate any possibility of the kidnappers using Ray's family as leverage; for instance, saying to Ray, "If you don't do as we ask, we'll do *this* to your wife and kids." Ray knew Wycliffe's policy of sending the family of a hostage back to the States, and therefore, would have known that any such threat would be a lie.

5. Billy Graham, *Unto the Hills* (Dallas: Word, 1993), 15.

Chapter 2: The Calling

1. An automatic rifle made in Israel.

2. A *caleta* is a bed, approximately twin-size, made from sticks and built a foot and a half above the ground. Covered with a mattress of chonta palm leaves, it is topped with a stick framework over which mosquito netting is draped and then crowned with a plastic tarp.

3. Originally the guerrillas took this knife away from Ray, but after he asked to borrow it many times over, they returned it to him.

4. "Ray of Lomalinda."

5. Pastusos are people from Pasto who speak an unusual dialect of Spanish and are often the brunt of jokes. The Paisas, from Antioquia, are known for their shrewd business activities.

6. FARC is the Spanish acronym for the Revolutionary Armed Forces of Colombia.

7. "Commit your way to the LORD, trust also in Him, and He shall bring it to pass. He shall bring forth your righteousness as the light, and your justice as the noonday. Rest in the LORD, and wait patiently for Him; do not fret because of him who prospers in his way, because of the man who brings wicked schemes to pass. Cease from anger, and forsake wrath; do not fret—it only causes harm" (NKJV).

8. Chaddy and Russell are the sons of Chad Stendal, a linguist and one of the founding members of Lomalinda. Longtime friends, Chad and Ray had worked together as leaders in the Boys' Brigade. The Stendals left SIL in 1974 but remained in the country. On August 14, 1983, Russell was kidnapped by the same guerrilla organization that abducted Ray. Through Chaddy's negotiation efforts for his brother's release, he gained considerable respect among the guerrillas. Russell was released on January 2, 1984. See *Rescue the Captors* by Russell Stendal, Ransom Press International, 1984; and *The Guerrillas Have Taken Our Son* by Chad and Pat Stendal, Ransom Press International, 1989 (10160 Main Drive, Bonita Springs, FL 34135).

9. While his overall physical strength improved due to the amount of exercise he sustained, Ray fought continuously with a fungus due to the moist jungle conditions (annual rainfall in the area where he was held averages well over one hundred inches).

10. Ray did not receive any of the letters Doris wrote to him.

Chapter 3: Looking Death in the Eye

1. Leo had had some medical training and was considered a "health promoter."

Chapter 4: Beside the River

1. Vinyl was used by the guerrillas to make pouches that were strung on their belts to carry ammunition. It was also used to construct back-

packs. Sewing the material together was done with a heavy needle and thread by holding the needle over a candle until hot, then pushing it through the vinyl. It was a slow procedure that produced lasting results.

2. The roof was a tarp strung between two trees on either side of the *caleta.*

3. With the exception of an expanded dialogue between the announcer and the translator—a friend of Doris's who had formerly worked in Colombia—and the lack of the Spanish translation, this comprises the actual transcript in its entirety (courtesy of SIL). Excerpts of the interview were aired twice daily from December 19 to December 24, 1994.

Chapter 5: The Holidays

1. Graham, *Unto the Hills,* 15.

Chapter 6: To Church

1. On January 31, 1993, Dave Mankins, Mark Rich, and Richard Tenenoff were kidnapped in Pucuro, Panama, and taken to Colombia, where they have been held hostage. As of this writing their fate is still unknown.

On January 16, 1994, Tim Van Dyke and Steve Welsh were taken captive near Villavicencio, Colombia. On June 19, 1995, they were both killed, presumably by cross fire between their captors and the Colombian military. See chapter 7, "Ups and Downs."

2. After nearly six weeks of captivity, Chet (Chester) Bitterman was shot in the chest on March 7, 1981, inside a chartered bus in Bogotá by members of the M-19—one of the most radical and unpredictable guerrilla groups in Colombia at the time. In exchange for Chet's life, the M-19 demanded that SIL withdraw from Colombia. After a decade of negative publicity from the press, Chet's death brought to SIL a flood of sympathy and approval from then-President Turbay on down to the common Colombian. See Steve Estes, *Called to Die* (Grand Rapids: Zondervan, 1986).

3. At age eighteen, Colombian boys must begin two years of military service.

4. Music from Valledupar in northern Colombia.

Chapter 7: Ups and Downs

1. By saying "the country of her origin," Lomalinda had given the guerrillas no real clue as to her whereabouts; though obviously American, her country of origin could be anywhere.

2. A *lapa* is a short-eared animal about the size of a small cocker spaniel and very tasty to eat.

3. A *gurri* is an armadillo. These are nocturnal animals that burrow in the ground, especially near water.

4. A *telenovela* is a TV novel, or soap opera. Most Colombian soap operas follow the standard themes of love, lust, envy, and hate, while others are endemic of the Colombian culture, revolving around "conflicts" between civilians, the military, and the guerrillas.

5. Horseflies are pesky insects that can bite through clothing, causing quite a sting.

6. Presumably, this letter from Ray, which his captors asked him to write (see chapter 7), was in response to the one written by the crisis committee and delivered to the guerrillas earlier that month.

Chapter 8: Justice and Mercy

1. "Be on your guard against men; they will hand you over to the local councils and flog you in their synagogues" (Matt. 10:17).

2. A type of constrictor, anacondas are very dangerous in the water. They have rows of spiny teeth that slant backward, and once they have bitten their victim, it is extremely difficult to pry them off.

3. A *torta* is fried batter similar to a doughnut.

4. Sunshine is a rare commodity for the guerrillas, who spend most of their time in the dense jungle areas where little light makes it past the thick canopy of trees.

Chapter 9: Deadly Games

1. A few of the guerrillas believed the reason why the surveillance planes followed them was because of Ray's supposed importance to the military.

2. When a Colombian says he is bored, it not only means he is weary of his current condition but that he intends to change it.

3. The guerrillas frequently read books for their indoctrination sessions. These included the writings of Karl Marx, histories of the Russian and Cuban revolutions, as well as biographies of dictators such as Stalin, Hitler, and Castro.

4. *Yamoo* is a large fish common to the region.

5. By this time Chaddy's contacts had also informed him that Ray, in fact, was alive. Although it is unknown why the guerrillas had lied, it is not uncommon for them to do so in hostage situations if they feel pres-

sure from the government or the military over the kidnapping. In such cases, feigning the hostage's death throws these entities off.

6. One of the constant problems of hostage negotiation in Colombia is not knowing for certain whether you are negotiating with the right party.

Chapter 10: The Long Haul

1. Any time a victim was to be shot, he was first blindfolded.

2. This guerrilla was José, who loved music and composed many of his own songs. See Chapter 5, "The Holidays."

3. The details of the agreement leading to Ray's release have not been included here to avoid interfering in any way with the ongoing investigation regarding the three New Tribes missionaries still believed to be held by guerrilla factions in Colombia.

Chapter 11: Release!

1. *Arrecife* is a reddish gray, lava-like gravel.

Conclusion: Illuminating the Path

1. See footnote 8 in chapter 2.

2. Ray learned later that at a school in Puerto Lleras, where he was well known among the children, a celebration was held the following day in which kids and adults alike wore placards announcing his release.

3. See *High Adventure in Colombia* by Chad Stendal, Ransom Press International, 1995 (10160 Main Drive, Bonita Springs, FL 34135).

Denise Marie Siino is a journalist and freelance writer who has written for such publications as the *Los Angeles Times, Charisma, Virtue,* and *Focus on the Family.* Siino resides in Santa Ana, California.